Contemporary
New Zealand
Plays

Contemporary New Zealand Plays

Selected and
introduced by
HOWARD McNAUGHTON

WELLINGTON
OXFORD UNIVERSITY PRESS
NEW YORK   LONDON   MELBOURNE

Oxford University Press, Ely House, W.1

GLASGOW NEW YORK TORONTO MELBOURNE WELLINGTON
CAPE TOWN IBADAN NAIROBI DAR ES SALAAM LUSAKA ADDIS ABABA
DELHI BOMBAY CALCUTTA MADRAS KARACHI LAHORE DACCA
KUALA LUMPUR SINGAPORE HONG KONG TOKYO

Oxford University Press, 66 Ghuznee St, Wellington

Introduction, selection and notes
© Oxford University Press 1974

First published 1974

ISBN 0 19 640015 5

Printed in Hong Kong by Peninsula Press Ltd.

CONTENTS

ACKNOWLEDGEMENTS

Grateful acknowledgement is made to Mrs Jacquie Baxter for permission to use *The Wide Open Cage,* and also to the individual authors of *When the Bough Breaks, Hongi* and *Salve Regina* for permission to include their works in this volume.

The verse quotations on pp. 69, 70, are from 'Miserere' by David Gascoyne, in *Collected Poems,* Oxford, in association with Andre Deutsch, London, 1965, pp. 40-41.

EDITOR'S NOTE

In preparing this volume, I have paid close attention to the results of a questionnaire sent to a number of people actively involved in New Zealand theatre and also to English teachers in schools and universities; their suggestions have been very helpful and have been followed as far as possible.

The editorial notes which precede the Campbell, Bowman, and Mason plays are partially derived from recorded interviews with the playwrights. Mr Phillip Mann and Unity Theatre have kindly allowed the reprinting of other notes. The shooting script extracts from *Salve Regina* have been generously provided by London Weekend Television, and for technical interpretation of these I am indebted to Mr Stan Hosgood of the N.Z.B.C. I am especially grateful to Mr William Austin, Head of Drama, N.Z.B.C., for his specially prepared notes on directing *Hongi*.

The Wide Open Cage was originally published in *Two Plays* by James K. Baxter (Capricorn Press, Hastings, 1959), and a slightly different version of *When the Bough Breaks* appeared in *Act,* July-September 1970; *Hongi* and *Salve Regina* have not been previously published.

INTRODUCTION

In 1971, a group of young actors who had trained in Jacques Lecoq's famous mime school in Paris arrived in New Zealand to work as a professional company; they called themselves 'Theatre Action', they scripted all their own material, and they seldom remained long in one place. New Zealand appealed to them because the absence of cultural traditions would allow them freedom that was not available in Paris, and the impact of their two-year survival supports their assumptions — an interesting demonstration that the 'weaknesses' of colonial cultures are not necessarily to the detriment of drama.

In fact, plays were being performed in New Zealand soon after the first ships arrived, and the first recorded performance of a locally-written play was thirteen years before the first New Zealand novel appeared. This early theatre had much in common with Theatre Action's methods, especially in the way it travelled to pubs, to goldfields, to wherever people were gathered together for any reason. Soon, however, large urban theatres appeared, and an Australasian circuit was established for professional companies; original material was frequently produced, though virtually no scripts survive apart from *The Land of the Moa* (1895), preserved in the Mitchell Library, Sydney. Certainly, most of the plays that were written for these companies seem to have been fairly stereotyped melodramas in line with contemporary European taste, but the fact remains that nineteenth-century New Zealand saw theatrical vigour on a scale that was not to be reached again until well into this century. And in one sense New Zealand was almost an ideal breeding-ground for melodrama, with its large population of drifters and adventurers who could easily be seen as picaresque drop-outs. The novelist William Satchell called the Hokianga gumfields 'The stranding-ground of the dead-beats of the world', and the potentiality for melodrama was there, if not the reality.

Melodrama went out of fashion at about the turn of the century. This was a world-wide trend, but it is obvious, too, that New Zealand had outgrown its social resources for melodrama. Elsewhere, naturalism and social drama were on the upsurge, but New Zealand found itself in an odd position: it had led the world in social advances, and this seems to have had a curiously neutralizing effect on its potential for social drama. Also, naturalism accentuated the intimacy of New Zealand society and brought an uncomfortable feeling of self-exposure; even in 1965, when New Zealand produced its first full-length television play (Bruce Mason's *The Evening Paper*), it was widely attacked for giving a false picture of New Zealand family life. There were other complications, too: the egalitarian image, the residual puritanism, and the consequent tendency towards introversion in local society brought something of a levelling-off of dramatic interest, as well as a limited scope for contrast and conflict.

Alan Mulgan appears to have been the first prominent New Zealand writer to attempt social drama after the style of Galsworthy, and by the thirties a torrent of similar plays was being written, encouraged by the establishment of the New Zealand branch of the British Drama League in 1932. However, reading through this material one gets a strong feeling that these dramatists had considerable difficulty finding much to write about and that, perhaps inevitably, they began to manufacture their own stereotypes; especially popular was the backblocks drama of the fight against falling prices, mortgages, isolation, animal disease, and droughts or floods.

Of course, this is to over-simplify the drama of the period: wherever Galsworthy turned, New Zealand dramatists happily followed, and he led them on a not uninteresting ramble. But there were two reasons why Galsworthy's drama could not develop very far in New Zealand. Firstly, New Zealand was a much looser society than contemporary Britain, so that, instead of men in conflict with men, local dramatists tended to have men interacting with their environment, and as the environment must necessarily be rather passive the outcome was often a piece of tidily 'well-made' dramatic convenience. And then there was the problem of speech: to make their characters dramatically viable, playwrights often had to make them over-articulate. At the time, the New Zealand Galsworthy cult seems to have been accepted quite easily, and it is obviously much the same thing as the colonial 'Home-complex' that coloured much prose writing in the twenties. But to find out how dramatically intractable much of the raw material of New Zealand life actually was between the wars, the reader has only to try dramatizing some of Frank Sargeson's early stories within naturalistic methods.

The answer, of course, lay in stylization. In 1972, the Amamus Players and the Court Theatre dramatized a number of local themes (including the depression and the temperance movement) within a documentary framework — a style, however, which really only began to evolve about 1945. On the other hand, the expressionist methods pioneered by Strindberg and the Germans had filtered through to America by the early twenties, and Eugene O'Neill and Elmer Rice made the style internationally known. It was only a matter of time before expressionism hit the New Zealand stage, and the first milestone came when the Canterbury Repertory Society (founded 1928) chose for its third production Capek's *R.U.R.,* the famous robot play.

Local playwrights seem to have been somewhat reluctant to move into expressionism, but two remarkable writers appeared in the thirties, both of whom were to have a long-term influence on New Zealand drama — Eric Bradwell and J.A.S. Coppard. Coppard had two of his plays, *Machine Song* and *Sordid Story,* included in an international anthology; he spent twelve years overseas, returned to work as a director in Auckland, and had two more expressionist plays, *Candy Pink* and *The Axe and the Oak Tree,* published in New Zealand in 1962. Bradwell became better known as a critic and administrator, but he wrote a lot of plays in the mid-thirties, one of which, *Clay,* was produced by the Thespians in the Wellington Concert Chamber in 1936. *Clay* is a fascinating and sophisticated piece of expressionism; its author seems to have understood the style very well, and the play remains one of those tantalizing high points which, if properly followed up, could have cut twenty years off the tortuous development of New Zealand drama.

Bradwell had found a style which was completely free from social and regional limitations, and it is sadly ironical that he chose to distance it by superfluous references to a European environment. Expressionistic drama, as Strindberg developed it, involved dramatizing the processes of a disordered mind; an obvious example would be *Alice's Adventures in Wonderland* translated into dramatic terms. The whole style is an attempt to probe beneath naturalistic externals to an area where superficial behavioural features are lost; time, location, the reliability of the senses, and often personal identity are blurred, distorted, or invalidated. Some of the stage directions to *Clay* suggest how it works:

The stage proper is divided into two sections, each of which is lit alternately as the play progresses. The left-hand section is draped in grey, and in front of the hangings is some sort of uneven mound, on and around which are grouped five creatures. They, too, are dressed in grey and are not unlike the conventional goblin. The whole scene should look as if it has been roughly modelled in clay. These five creatures, in their setting, represent the woman's mind, and utter the incoherent and fleeting thoughts that are tormenting her.

It will be seen that this is essentially the same concept of dramaturgy as that behind *When the Bough Breaks,* though of course

11

the two plays have little else in common. *Clay* represented an advance in New Zealand writing which paralleled the work that Frank Sargeson was doing in the short story at the same time. New Zealand drama had found a method by which even the most inarticulate introvert in Sargeson's stories might be projected on to the stage, but it was to be a long time before this possibility was explored.

In the post-war period, a comparison between Australian and New Zealand drama becomes pertinent. Both countries produced outstanding poetic drama, in particular that of Allen Curnow (*The Axe*, 1946) and Douglas Stewart, but it was not until the mid-fifties that a strong, continuing tradition of local play-writing began in both countries. Australia saw the spectacular successes of Ray Lawler (*Summer of the Seventeenth Doll*, 1955) and Alan Seymour (*The One Day of the Year*, 1961), both writing in a semi-naturalistic vein, and this became so firmly established that it was able to swamp the expressionistic masterpieces that Patrick White wrote in the early sixties (*The Season at Sarsaparilla*, 1962; *A Cheery Soul*, 1963). New Zealand, on the other hand, has never had a really successful naturalistic play. One New Zealander, Merton Hodge, wrote a number of plays in the thirties, one of which (*The Wind and the Rain*) ran for three years in the West End; most of his work was in the realistic, 'well-made' style that was then in vogue, but it was all very heavily directed towards British commercial production and had relatively little attention here.

Merton Hodge and Bruce Mason both returned to New Zealand soon after the war; Hodge took a medical practice in Dunedin and died there in 1958 after trying unsuccessfully to get some of his own later work staged. Bruce Mason, on the other hand, began writing plays as a reaction against what he had seen in the West End; by the time of Hodge's death, Mason had established himself as New Zealand's first really professional playwright, and in his mature work he has moved even further away from naturalism. Mason has a highly-developed sense of dramatic shape, and this, as much as anything, seems to have influenced his later style.

One of the most noticeable things about New Zealand drama between 1945 and 1965 is the recurrence of names that are better known in other literary fields: Curnow, Campbell, Dibble, Baxter, Cresswell, Sargeson, Bland, and numerous others. Mason is probably the only major playwright in the period with an obvious sense of vocation, and it is significant that he has almost always written with specific production conditions in mind. His early plays were British Drama League material, and by the time he did the final drafts of

The Pohutukawa Tree he knew it was to be done by Richard Campion's (professional) New Zealand Players. His later pieces for solo theatre were written for Wellington's Downstage Theatre, and most of his Maori plays (including *Hongi*) were originally for the New Zealand Broadcasting Corporation (N.Z.B.C.). Mason's success in the early sixties was sensational, especially with *The Pohutukawa Tree* and *The End of the Golden Weather;* certainly, they aroused plenty of criticism, but his energy and persistence gave a much-needed lead to other dramatists.

At the same time, the N.Z.B.C. was beginning to produce New Zealand drama on an appreciable scale: in 1960 it produced thirteen locally-written plays, in 1965 it accepted forty-six. Almost all recent New Zealand playwrights have had some of their early work produced by the N.Z.B.C., and it is obvious that the flexibility of the radio medium has led some of them to technical experimentation on stage. New Zealand radio has served as a melting-pot which has absorbed novels, short stories, poetry, and documentary material and transmuted them into dramatic shape, sometimes to reappear on stage. Janet Frame's novel *A State of Siege* has been adapted for stage and radio by Rosalie Carey of Dunedin's Globe Theatre (where Baxter's later plays were mostly premièred). Mason's *The End of the Golden Weather,* a work for solo theatre which he has done about six hundred times, originated from a series of radio talks about his childhood. Alistair Campbell had a poetic sequence, *Sanctuary of Spirits,* produced as a kind of radio verse drama before he even wrote his first play, *The Homecoming,* also for radio, and loosely based on material from his own diary. The radio drama department of the N.Z.B.C. has provided a sympathetic and well-paying outlet to all New Zealand writers, and it holds easily the best single collection of recent New Zealand drama.

Stage production, being relatively uncoordinated and lacking much financial security, has until recently lagged behind radio. The New Zealand Theatre Federation (incorporating the local branch of the British Drama League) offers numerous trophies for local work, but has tended to attract a rather stereotyped kind of product; in the early seventies, though, the Federation has taken on a much more forward-looking appearance, with liberal, experimental plays winning various competitions.

The professional companies which have arisen since the mid-sixties have all produced New Zealand plays, though Wellington's Downstage has easily the most impressive record, with thirteen New Zealand plays in its first fifty productions; *Salve*

Regina and *When the Bough Breaks* both had experimental, low-budget seasons at Downstage in late 1969. Auckland's Mercury has done an impressive, full-scale production of James McNeish's *The Rocking Cave,* and Mervyn Thompson, director of Christchurch's Court Theatre, has scripted and produced *O! Temperance,* a documentary play which has been very successful at the Court and also on tour. There are numerous companies which draw on a smaller amount of professionalism and have low-capacity theatres; consequently, they can afford a more adventurous programme. Chief among these is Dunedin's Globe Theatre, where Patric Carey produced many of Baxter's plays. Unity Theatre (Wellington), Central Theatre (Auckland), and the Elmwood Players (Christchurch) all have noteworthy records of producing local plays.

Since about 1965, a very strong group of younger playwrights has appeared, characterised by a professional seriousness that was very rare a decade earlier; they have all worked mainly through the N.Z.B.C. and the new professional companies. Joseph Musaphia (who actually had one play, *Free,* produced by the New Zealand Theatre Trust in 1961), Peter Bland, Max E. Richards, Anthony Taylor, and Robert Lord have looked the most promising of these. Lord began to attract attention only in 1972 with *Meeting Place* at Downstage (directed by Anthony Taylor), and a year later already had an impressive production record on stage, radio, and television.

In May, 1973, nine professional or semi-professional productions of New Zealand plays were running throughout the country, and almost all of them were attracting very good houses. Ten years before, few of the companies even existed, and the only professional outlet for scripts was the N.Z.B.C. The Queen Elizabeth II Arts Council has been actively encouraging high-quality productions of local plays, and the N.Z.B.C. has been offering very competitive rates: in 1972, it was possible for a playwright to earn a salary slightly above the national average by selling six sixty-minute plays to the N.Z.B.C.

The four plays in this collection have been chosen primarily for their individual merits, but they also give a broad sampling of the diversity of recent New Zealand play-writing. Interestingly, they all turn out to have related themes. *The Wide Open Cage* and *Salve Regina* are both, in different senses, 'drop-out dramas.' *Hongi* and *When the Bough Breaks* both involve racial issues to some degree, and *Hongi* and *Salve Regina* are basically about a reversion to savagery. *When the Bough Breaks* and *The Wide Open Cage* both raise questions of confinement and poetic release from the flesh.

Hongi and *The Wide Open Cage* take radically different approaches to the central issue of human stature: Hongi is a colossus, Baxter's characters are stunted men. But although the same general themes recur, their treatment is strikingly dissimilar: stylistically, all of these plays are strongly individual, asserting their own issues within their own terms.

Alistair Te Ariki Campbell is best known as a poet, and so it is not altogether surprising that four of his five plays are strikingly subjective, exploring different types of expressionism. *When the Bough Breaks* is his only stage play, and was based on his first radio play, *The Homecoming.* As he sees it, adaptation for stage made the play 'centripetal rather than linear in development,' and the characters 'tend to be extensions of Kate's states of mind rather than characters in their own right.' This comes close to Strindberg's use of expressionism as a kind of ego-radiation, and it must be stressed that *When the Bough Breaks* is not a naturalistic play: Campbell is dramatizing a mind in anguish (with the distortion and confusion that implies), and the whole action of the play takes place in Kate's mind while she is in a mental hospital. Kate is not a narrator — she is more of a *lens,* and her delirious vision is not presented as a reliable reflection of events leading up to her illness. Everything is coloured by her mental state; as Matt points out, she tends to see herself as a melodramatic heroine, and it is appropriate that some minor characters should be distorted almost into types. The subjective structure gives this play an extraordinary fluidity, rather like a poem; Kate's delirium liberates her from both time and location. On the other hand, the confusion of a chronological sense means that causation is very difficult to unravel. The origins of Kate's illness and its consequences are obscure; there is no attempt to plot them with a clinical tidiness. Partly, this is because the origins of mental illness *are* a complex business, but it is also because we are asked to share the nightmare from the inside, not scrutinise it from the bedside.

Phillip Mann, director of the first production of *When the Bough Breaks,* had this to say in his notes on the staging of the play:

Such is the structure of the play that the lighting is of central importance. It should suggest the fluid movement of the play both from scene to scene and back and forth in time. It should interpret, through angle, colour, intensity, and shadow the different qualities of the scenes. It should be incisive and muscular, and not a timid device used only so that the audience can see. I feel that the lighting should be keyed to rhythms in the text. . . . Essentially what one needs is a neutral space, which can be defined by the light. We did find

17

that variations in level gave an extraordinary power to the scenes which are not set in any one specific location. An excess of setting would, I feel, detract from the speedy action of the play.

In our production, the minor parts were shared between three actors. While this was at first making a virtue of necessity, we did find that this lent concentration to the main characters and increased the comparative unreality of the minor characters. They were thumbnail sketches next to portraits. We found it essential that the minor parts have a clarity of characterisation, at times bordering on caricature.

— from *Act* 11, July-September 1970.

Alistair Campbell's other plays are: *The Homecoming* (1964), *The Proprietor* (1965), *The Suicide* (1965), *The Wairau Incident* (1969). *When the Bough Breaks* was finished in 1969.

CRITICAL ARTICLES

FRASER, IAN. 'The Gulbenkian Theatre: Two Plays'.
   Landfall XXIV, 94 (1970), 164-69.

McNAUGHTON, HOWARD. 'The Plays of Alistair Campbell'.
   Landfall XXVIII, 109 (1974).

ALISTAIR CAMPBELL

When the Bough Breaks

Characters

MATT, *Part-Maori, 33*
KATE, 20
DR WARNER, Psychiatrist
NURSING SISTER
MOTHER
FATHER
GRANDFATHER
COLIN, 33
RALPH, 25
JILL, 30
FEMALE PATIENT, 50
CHAIRWOMAN
GIRL

SCENE ONE

Sound effects, suggestive of rasping, gasping breathing begins faintly but gradually increases in volume as KATE fades up, sitting on a chair, front centre, breathing in time to them.
Sound effects cut out and rooster crows, breaking KATE's trance.

KATE: Three o'clock. *(Clock strikes three. Consults her watch.)* Right on time as usual. *(Rooster crows.)* Crow on, little cock — but much good will it do you! For no one believes you even exist — least of all Matt. It's all in my head, he says. I've a cock in my head! At three in the morning he wakes me without fail. It's always bad at that hour. In the dark night of the soul, it is always three o'clock in the morning. Did I read that somewhere? Matt will know. I must ask him. *(Worried)* But where is he? Why doesn't he come? It's so late. *(Walks round distractedly and calls out.)* Matt — where are you, dear?

Sound of laughter, low at first, but mounting as MATT and GIRL come into view, centre.

I miss you. I'm so lonely. Please come home. Matt — where are you? *(Bitterly)* Drinking with your friends, no doubt! Chatting up some university trollop!

Shriek of laughter from the GIRL, as MATT drunkenly embraces her and tries to kiss her.

KATE goes up to them and screams out.

Stop it!

The couple disengage in surprise, then fade out.

Oh, you men! You're all the same — and we women are no better! You kick us in the fanny and we come cringing back — and all for a cock in the bed! *(Rooster crows.)* Cock in the head — a cocked-up head! *(Holds her head.)* Oh, my poor noodle!

Fade in WARNER in position.

How you can stand it, I don't know! It's these nightmares — they're getting worse. I dread going to bed at night — and my heart, it pounds and pounds. I'm terrified of a heart attack. *(Listlessly, as she sits down)* I had another nightmare last night.

WARNER: Tell me about it.
KATE: *(Turning round, startled)* Doctor? Dr Warner?

WARNER: Tell me about your nightmare.

KATE: *(Nervously)* I was in a house. It was large, but the walls were thin, flimsy, like — like the sides of a matchbox. It was dark — very dark. Outside, something was trying to get in. I don't know what it was, except it was huge and black, like a bear — a huge black bear. I went from room to room, looking for a way to escape — but wherever I went, there it was, huge and black, blocking the window with its body, and . . . feeling about inside with a huge paw — as if trying to find *me*. I — I think I screamed. Anyway, I was suddenly wide awake — and my husband was bending over me . . . huge and black against the moon. And his hands . . .

WARNER: Yes?

KATE: Were on my throat.

WARNER: *(Sceptically)* Hmmm. Your husband is a Maori, isn't he?

KATE: You know he is.

WARNER: Does his colour bother you?

KATE: I love him!

WARNER: That's not what I asked.

KATE: I don't understand.

WARNER: Don't you?

KATE goes up to WARNER aggressively.

KATE: What are you driving at? *(Furiously)* He tried to strangle me. You pompous fool! Get that into your thick skull — he tried to strangle me!

Fade down WARNER.

SCENE TWO

Sudden transition, accompanied by light change, to MATT and SISTER, standing in their positions, MATT holding flowers.

KATE immediately sees MATT and gasps in terror.

KATE: *(Flinching)* Don't do it, Matt. Don't do it . . . Don't do it . . .

SISTER: You have a visitor, Mrs Thompson.

MATT: *(Steps forward, uncertainly)* How are you, Kate? I came to see you. I — I brought you flowers. *(Holds them out.)*

KATE takes the flowers and turns away, holding them to her face.

21

They're wild flowers. I thought you'd like them.

KATE: I love them.

MATT tries to kiss her, but KATE turns her face away.

No — don't kiss me. My mouth tastes awful.

SISTER: Try not to upset her, Mr Thompson. *(Goes out.)*

KATE: Matt?

MATT: Yes, Kate.

KATE: We've done an awful thing.

MATT: What do you mean?

KATE: Breaking up your marriage — taking Simon away from his mother. What kind of future can *he* expect? He should be with his mother, Matty.

MATT: It's too late for that.

KATE: But is it? Can't we at least discuss it?

MATT: Discuss it? Christ — we've done nothing else for weeks!

KATE: Matt — there's something you ought to know. I didn't tell you earlier because I knew how upset you would be. It's about Simon.

MATT: Go on.

KATE: It's the old story of the wicked stepmother. I can't do a thing with him. He doesn't do anything very bad — just a number of little things which all add up to another big headache for me.

MATT: Is he jealous of the baby?

KATE: Jealous of Mary? He has no reason to be. I mean, I do all sorts of little things for him.

MATT: What he needs is a warm hug now and then to make him feel part of the family.

KATE: But I do hug him lots of times — whenever I can get away from Mary.

MATT: But you still feel Simon should be with his mother?

KATE: Yes, I do. I think every child should be with the mother who bore him. Only she can give him the love he really needs.

MATT: You feel you can't love him enough, is that it?

KATE: *(Irritated)* What are you driving at? Are you suggesting I'm depriving your precious son of affection? *(Throws down flowers.)*

MATT picks up the flowers and puts them on KATE's chair.

MATT: I'm sorry. Forget it. It's not turning out much of a visit, is it?

KATE: I didn't ask you to come — *(softening)* but I'm glad you came. Matt?

She stretches her hand towards MATT, then stiffens, her eyes widening with horror.

MATT: What's the matter?
KATE: *(Shuddering)* Can't you see? Can't you smell? *(Looks with loathing at herself.)* I'm so filthy! *(Sharply, as he makes a move towards her)* Keep away from me. I'm not fit for human contact.
MATT: Don't blame yourself too much. Everything's a mess at the moment, but —
KATE: But what, Matty? *(Sits down on the sofa.)*
MATT: Oh, I don't know . . . I feel that good will come of it.
KATE: *(Drily)* What is goodness, Matty? Is breaking up a marriage goodness? Is breaking a little boy's heart goodness? Our little baby — is she goodness? *(Vehemently)* No, no no — she's the fruit of evil behaviour! Daddy says the children of mixed marriages inherit the worst features of both races. How right he is — dear Daddy! I should have listened to him. *(Bitterly)* But I listened to you instead — *(hissing the words out)* the voice of the serpent.

KATE pauses, her eyes growing wide with panic.

MATT: *(Exasperated)* What's the matter now?
KATE: My baby — where's my baby?
MATT: Oh, for God's sake — cut out the melodrama!
KATE: My baby!
MATT: Look, Kate — she's all right. Jill's looking after her. You know that. *(KATE wails.)* Listen to me — Mary's all right. *(Sharply)* Kate! *(Bends over her.)*
KATE: *(Flinching)* Daddy — don't hurt me. I'll be good.
MATT: *(Shaking her gently)* Kate, it's me — Matt. Please tell me what's wrong. *(Sits down beside her.)*
KATE: *(Coming out of trance)* Matty. *(Throwing her arms round him in relief)* It's you. Where am I?
MATT: You're in hospital, Kate. You're going to be all right. Just take it easy.
KATE: I'm never going to get better, Matt. I know that now.
MATT: Don't talk nonsense.
KATE: *(Calmly)* It's not nonsense. I know what I'm talking about. I can never come back to you. *(Theatrically)* I am lost to you forever! *(Pause)* Matty? Say something. *(Puts her hand on his sleeve.)*

MATT: *(Snatching his arm away)* Know what I'm thinking — do you?

KATE: Don't let's quarrel — not here. I feel sick.

MATT: Sick my foot! I think you're shirking.

KATE: I want to go home.

MATT: Yeah — I really think you're shirking.

KATE: Please — let me go home to my parents.

MATT: Know what else I think? I think you're just plain gutless — yeah, just plain bloody gutless. You haven't the guts to face up to your responsibilities — so you're playing sick. *(Shouts.)* Do you hear me?

KATE: *(Helplessly)* No — no —

MATT: You're play-acting! *(Mimics her.)* Daddy, Daddy! You make me sick!

KATE: Poor Daddy — he's an old man!

MATT: He's an old bastard! *(Mutters angrily.)* Oh — what's the use? Sometimes I don't know *who's* crazy — you or me.

KATE: *(Quietly)* I know.

MATT: Stop it — do you hear? I can't take any more. I'm fed up to the teeth. I'm bored with you — bored with your sickness — bored with your stuck-up family. You know what? They think you've chucked yourself away on a no-good Maori boy — and, what's more, an educated Maori boy — an intellectual snob. Well, they can have you back for nothing. *(Shouts.)* You're punk, do you hear?

KATE: *(Moaning)* No, Matt — no!

MATT: Punk, punk, punk! Punk wife, punk mother, punk actress, punk human being! You're even a punk maniac!

Shocked silence, as KATE walks dejectedly to her chair, picks up the flowers and sits down.

KATE: *(Quietly)* What can I say, except I'm sorry? Everything's gone wrong. It's always been like that as long as I remember. You're right. I *am* punk. And I'm ignorant and stupid. But do you know what?

MATT: *(Sullenly)* What?

KATE: Apart from you my life would be less than nothing. Do you know what kept me going all those terrible days? The thought of your return each evening. I used to live for the sound of your footsteps round the side of the house . . . Matt, you want your freedom, don't you? I can't stop you. I've no right to stop you. *(Voice breaking)* Oh, Matty — we're finished, aren't we? *(Begins to weep.)* You've been seeing Sally again, haven't you? Matt —

24

look at me. I'm no use any more. I'll be here for the rest of my life. Sally is strong and healthy — and I know she loves you. She'll be a good mother to the children — much better than I'll ever be. Matty dear — take the children away and start again . . .

SISTER returns.

SISTER: *(Briskly)* Well, we mustn't tire her, must we, Mr Thompson?

MATT: *(Intensely)* Kate — listen to me. No matter what happens, I will never leave you — not for Sally or anyone else.

SISTER: *(Reaching for the flowers)* I'll take these, dear.

KATE: *(Suddenly furious)* Give them back. Give them back to me.

KATE snatches at the flowers and, when she misses, she strikes at the SISTER, who wards off the blow.

SISTER ⎫   That'll do, Mrs Thompson!
⎬ : *(Together)*
MATT ⎭   For God's sake, Kate!

SISTER: *(Sternly)* Come along, Mr Thompson.

MATT: Goodbye, Kate. *(Tries to kiss her, but she averts her face.)*

KATE: If you love me, you will stay with me. *(Calls after him tragically.)* But I love you . . . I love you . . . I love you . . .

Slow fade SISTER and MATT, as they walk upstage, talking quietly, to take up their positions, facing the audience. WARNER also moves into position.

MATT: I'm sorry that happened.

SISTER: So am I, Mr Thompson. We might have to put her in a single room.

MATT: She won't like that.

SISTER: It's for her own good.

SCENE THREE

Change of light to synchronise with KATE's change of character. As she swings round to the audience, MATT, the SISTER and WARNER snap to attention.

KATE: You may not believe this, but I'm really sane *(gets up)* — which is more than you can say for my husband. *(Walks up to MATT)* Poor Matt — he's been hopelessly insane for years! And that creature over there *(gesturing)* — she's mad, too. And Dr Warner — quite, quite mad. If only I knew where the uniforms were kept, I'd pass myself off as a nurse, and no one would know. *(Wistfully)* I'd be a nice nurse. I wouldn't ever be bossy. *(Shrewdly)* I know what you're thinking. If she's sane, as she claims to be, how come she's locked up in a nut house? A good question — but I can answer it. My dear, loving husband committed me. Why? Simple. He knew I was worried about his health and thought I was scheming to have *him* committed. So, he got in first. The dirty dog! I hate him. I hate him!

The others take up her cry, like a Greek chorus, repeating it, one after the other, to create a surging, rhythmical effect, which tears at KATE's nerves. She turns to them and screams out.

No!

The chorus cuts out instantly. The SISTER and WARNER now go out.

That's not true, I love him — Oh, God, I love him! *(Turns to the audience.)* Don't you believe me? We used to be very much in love. You still don't believe me, do you? Very well, you asked for it.

SCENE FOUR

Sudden cross-fade to MATT, sitting in his position and leaning back on an elbow. He is looking across at KATE and laughing.

MATT: How does making love feel to a man? Nice.

KATE: Is that all? Just — nice? *(Sits beside him.)* It doesn't seem fair, considering how much pleasure a woman gets.

MATT: And when it's over, some men have a feeling of revulsion —

KATE: You don't feel like that afterwards, do you? I'd be terribly hurt, if you did.

MATT: I told you: I feel nice. It's a strong word in my vocabulary. I think *you're* nice.

They kiss long and tenderly, then fall apart, smiling at each other.

MATT: All right?

KATE: *(Stretching with pleasure)* Hmmm — lovely. It makes my toes curl up. Do you love me?

MATT: What a question! *(Rises and comes forward.)* I love this girl. *(Lyrically)* I love her in a green tree, with white birds passing over,

26

white clouds passing over. I love her in the light and in the darkness — light in the darkness, darkness in the light. I love her time out of mind, mind out of time. I love her in a red chair, holding a white rose. I love her smiling, as I take my black sword and plunge it into her red, red rose. *(Slides his hand up her dress.)*

KATE: *(Jumping)* Your hand's cold!

MATT laughs and strokes her knee.

MATT: Knees are sweet,
      ankles, too.
      Open knees —
      and I love you.
(Lyrically) As the apple reddens and falls, I love this girl. As the black water takes the apple and circles widen, I love this girl. As her lips are red and her teeth are white and the apple is sweet, I love this girl. As the juices flow and commingle, and love is sweet and love is sweet, I love this girl. *(Kisses her lightly on the brow.)*

KATE: I love you!

MATT: How about marrying me?

KATE: *(Catches her breath)* Are you proposing to me?

MATT: What does it sound like?

KATE: I don't know. Like — like saying to a friend: 'How about coming to the pub?' Do you mean it?

MATT: Of course I do! I want to make a virtuous woman of you. And there's bound to be a baby —

KATE: *(Quickly)* You don't think I'm pregnant, do you?

MATT: What do you say?

KATE rises, face alight, and walks about, as if on air.

KATE: Ever since I first met you I've been saying yes. At first it was my body, but now it's all of me saying yes. People's bodies are so much wiser than their minds. People should always listen to what their bodies say. When we first met, my body said yes so openly I was scared you might think I was throwing myself at you.

MATT: But you looked so demure — virginal almost. You hardly raised your eyes. But you're right. I did feel something. I wanted to touch you, but you were surrounded by all those people. You looked sexy and chaste at the same time. I think that's what intrigued me most about you. I watched you all evening. Did you know that?

KATE: I think I did — but I can't be sure. I think my body knew, because all of a sudden I became light-hearted and breathless. I became very gay and talkative.

MATT: I know. That's when I became depressed. As long as you were quiet and mouse-like, I thought I had a chance with you. You see — I had designs on you even then. No, that's not quite true. Something extraordinary was going on between us. Tenderness is not something I often feel, but that evening I felt tender towards you.

KATE: But you barely spoke to me. When you came over and we were introduced, you hardly said a word. I thought I'd offended you, because suddenly you muttered something and walked away. Why did you do that? I wanted to run after you, but my pride wouldn't let me. Why did you walk out on me?

MATT: Because I knew I'd found you. I was afraid.

KATE: But why?

MATT: You were so beautiful . . . I don't know. I felt inadequate.

KATE: You shouldn't have walked out on me. I felt very sad. Anyway, it doesn't matter now. And then that weekend at the pub. We were together, and nothing else seemed to matter.

MATT: And the waitress —

KATE: *(Laughing)* Oh, yes! She knew we weren't married. I practically waved my borrowed wedding-ring under her nose — but she wasn't to be fooled. How do you think she knew?

MATT: It was that gym frock you were wearing.

KATE: It wasn't a gym frock.

MATT: It was so. Don't argue with me. I'm an expert on the subject. Anyway, I didn't like it, so I took it off you — and I don't remember you protesting.

KATE: How could I? You're much stronger than I . . . And afterwards, when you were asleep, I cried.

MATT: I didn't know that. Why did you cry?

KATE: For happiness, for your poor wife — I don't know. All night long the trains clanked past and the cistern gurgled, and I lay awake staring into the darkness. I don't know why I was worried. Yes, I do. Something seemed to hang over us. It was full of menace.

KATE rises and moves slowly forward.

MATT: Public opinion, I suspect.

The clock strikes three and they freeze. On the third chime, KATE moves forward again.

KATE: Don't let's talk about it. It's much too late. *(Raising her voice)* Thank you for that weekend. It was beautiful. For three nights I lay in your arms —

MATT: I love you!

KATE: *(Challengingly)* Is it wrong to snatch at happiness?

SCENE FIVE

Sudden transition to MOTHER and FATHER standing in their positions. MOTHER immediately starts speaking.

MOTHER: It must be a white wedding, of course.

KATE: Mother, please —

MOTHER: And I have seen just the dress for you. And, of course, the veil — I've kept it all these years. It was mine — and my mother's before me.

KATE: Mummy, please listen. Matt and I want to get married in a Registry Office.

MOTHER: What nonsense, dear! No, I have it all planned. A big church wedding and reception. My goodness — the reception. Where are we going to hold it? We can't hold it here. There's no room. What a pity, because the garden has never been lovelier. Oh, well!

KATE: Oh dear! I don't know what Matt will think.

FATHER: *(Turning sharply)* What's all the excitement?

MOTHER: Now, the guests. There'll be at least 500 guests —

FATHER: Will someone kindly tell me what's going on?

MOTHER: ... And champagne. We can run to champagne, can't we darling? It's not every day your daughter gets married.

FATHER: What?

MOTHER: Everyone that's anyone must be there. It will be the biggest, loveliest wedding of the year!

FATHER: And the most expensive! Do I know him?

MOTHER: Of course you know him! *(Stops, puzzled.)* Katie dear ... who are you going to marry? You haven't told me.

KATE: I've tried to tell you, Mummy — but you got carried away. His name is Matthew Thompson.

MOTHER: Matthew Thompson.

FATHER: Matthew Thompson. The name rings a bell. He's a bank clerk, isn't he?

MOTHER: *(Laughs scornfully)* Our Katie marrying a bank clerk!

The following dialogue must be rapid-fire.

FATHER: A dentist then?

KATE: No.

MOTHER: An accountant?

KATE: No.

FATHER: A lawyer?

KATE: No.

MOTHER: A doctor?

KATE: No.

FATHER: A stockbroker?

KATE: *(Shouts)* No! He's a poet. *(Shocked silence)* And he's a Maori!

MOTHER: *(Outraged)* What?

FATHER My God — now I've heard the lot. *My* daughter marrying a bloody Maori!

MOTHER: Please, darling — it doesn't help to swear. *(Tearful)* Oh, Katie — how could you do this to us after all we've done for you? We've tried to bring you up decently. We sent you to the best schools —

FATHER: Cost a packet. I can tell you!

MOTHER: And the university —

FATHER: And this is all the thanks we get!

MOTHER: How can I hold my head up among the neighbours?

FATHER: Give him up, Kate. It wouldn't work. You'd be marrying problems.

MOTHER: Listen to your father, dear. He knows best.

FATHER: I tell you what. Business has been very good. We'll go abroad — England, the Continent — anywhere you like . . .

MOTHER: Would you like that, Kate?

FATHER: You'll soon forget him.

MOTHER: There are lots of nice young men. You could have the pick of them.

FATHER: We're wasting time. She was always pig-headed. A black tracker, my God!

MOTHER: I blame the university. She should never have gone there.

FATHER: It was your idea.

MOTHER: I beg your pardon! It was your idea —

KATE loses self-control, covers her ears and screams out.

KATE: Shut up! I love him! Can't you understand? I love him!

Black out.

30

SCENE SIX

Gasping sound effects, quiet at first, start immediately the light goes out and mount steadily through the scene. Fade up KATE to very dim. She is feeling her way round a small room that the audience has to imagine is there.

KATE: *(Frightened)* Where am I?

She finds the back wall and then feels round to find one of the side walls.

Where have they put me?

Moves round to front wall — the wall nearest to audience. Shows relief, as she finds the door.

The door! *(Feels up and down it.)* No handle! *(Growing panic)* There's no door handle! Oh, God — where have they put me? *(Shouts.)* Sister! *(Listens.)* Sister — let me out! *(Listens again.)* *(Panics.)* Oh, God — God! *(Beats the door with her fists.)* Let me out — let me out — let me out —

MOTHER takes up her cry, quietly at first and mounting in volume.

(Shouts desperately) Stop!

Sound effects and MOTHER immediately cut out.

I can't stand it — I can't stand it — I can't stand it —

Footsteps start quietly, growing louder, as they approach. They stop outside the door.

KATE freezes, then asks quaveringly.

Sister?

A rattle of keys, a key turns in the lock and the door creaks open.

KATE shows extreme terror. She backs away and screams out.

No! No! *NO!*

Black out.

31

SCENE SEVEN

Fade up slowly KATE sprawled on her stomach on the floor, with PATIENT, staring down at her and shaking her head.

KATE at last becomes aware of her and sits up.

PATIENT: You've been a naughty girl. Tut, tut! You've been carrying on like nobody's business. You made Sister very cross. But she's forgiven you — she let you out. You were shut away, you know.

KATE: *(Groaning)* My head!

PATIENT: Shock treatment, dearie.

KATE: *(Rising)* Who are you?

PATIENT: Mind your own business. Got a fag?

KATE: Sorry — don't smoke.

PATIENT: Oh, well — have to smoke me own then. *(Takes a butt from her pocket and lights up.)*

KATE: Why are *you* here?

PATIENT: Same reason as you, dearie. I'm mad. What a question! *(Nudges KATE.)* Hey — that young man who comes to visit you: is he your husband?

KATE: Yes, he is.

PATIENT: Handsome, isn't he?

KATE: *(Pleased)* Do you think so?

PATIENT: Bet he's hot stuff. You can tell when a man's hot stuff. It's in the way he walks.

KATE: *(Laughs.)* How do you mean?

PATIENT: He walks as if his pants are on fire. He can share my bed any time he wants to. *(Cackles until she chokes and splutters.)* No harm meant, dearie. We get pretty sex-starved in here, as you'll find out soon enough. *(Puffs away thoughtfully.)* Was that your mother visiting you this afternoon?

KATE: Yes.

PATIENT: All she needs is a good fuck. *(Shocked exclamation from KATE)* But Old Dryballs, who was with her — he's not the one to do it. He couldn't, if he tried.

KATE: *(Outraged)* You're talking about my father!

PATIENT: Bet they haven't slept together for years.

KATE: Stop talking like that!

PATIENT: Never liked him from the moment I first clapped eyes on him. The way he struts about! What's he done to be so proud about? He's nothing.

KATE: Stop it. I say!

32

PATIENT: *(Surprised)* He put you here, didn't he?

KATE: You're wrong. My husband put me here.

PATIENT: I'm not wrong, dearie. I'm never wrong. What sort of man is he to treat his daughter like that — his *own* daughter? By crikey — he's a queer one! *(Cackles.)* Well, dearie — I'm off to cadge a smoke. Ta ta.

SCENE EIGHT

Cross-fade to MATT and COLIN, sitting in MATT's position, laughing and swigging from a bottle of beer, which they pass from one to the other.

COLIN: Remember those two factory sheilas we picked up?

MATT: Do I what? *(Laughs.)* I tried to soften my one up with verse.

COLIN: Latin verse! She was wide open for a good plain Maori boy, but you spouting Propertius — that scared the tits off her!

MATT: I was pretty weird in those days.

COLIN: You were a bloody romantic, living in the wrong age. Christ — I nearly pissed myself when you gave a kind of strangled cry and flung yourself at her. *(Laughs.)* She was out of that room so fast she left her pants behind. *(Suddenly serious)* Anyway — good to see you, boy. How are things?

MATT: Great — terrific! For the first time in my life, I'm sexually satisfied!

COLIN: *(Drily)* Yeah — that's important, of course. You and your wife didn't hit it off, so you're determined to make a go of it with Kate. Fair enough, too. Come back in a year's time and tell me you're happy and I'll say, 'Good on you — you've made a go of it!' The ideal situation, as I see it, is this *(extending his hand, palm upwards, fingers straight):* the unclenched fist. No tension — everything open and above board. Know what I mean?

MATT: Yeah.

COLIN: But let's face it. Sex is a drug — like booze. At first it relieves tension, but, if you have too much of it, it increases tension — unless the relationship is like this. *(Extends his hand, as before.)*

MATT: *(Ironically)* The unclenched fist!

COLIN: *(Laughs)* Good on you! *(Gets up, clutching the bottle.)* Well — got to get moving. Got some unfinished business — a little Irish Catholic girl who's keeping it on ice for her boy friend. But I'm working on her. *(Goes out.)*

33

MATT: Good luck.

COLIN: *(Calls back)* The same to you! *(Fading)* Come back in a
year's time . . .

Fade down MATT, staring at his unclenched fist.

SCENE NINE

Fade up MOTHER and FATHER, still in their positions.

FATHER: Is he after my money, do you think?

MOTHER: We're losing our daughter — and all you think about is
your money!

FATHER: Well, he won't see a cent of it — not a cent!

*Fade up MATT standing erect in his position and KATE in her
chair. As he speaks, MATT slowly comes forward.*

MATT: Blue rain from a clear sky.
Our world a cube of sunlight —
but to the south
the violet admonition
of thunder.

Innocent as flowers,
your eyes with their thick lashes,
open in green surprise.

What have we to fear?
Frost and a sharp wind
reproach us,
and a tall sky pelts the roof
with blue flowers.

MATT stands alongside KATE.

KATE: You and I in bed, my love.

MATT: heads leaning together,

KATE: merry as thieves

MATT: eating stolen honey —

MATT ⎫
KATE ⎬ : *(Together)* what have we to fear
⎭   but a borrowed world
                      collapsing all about us
                      in blue ruins?

MOTHER: *(Cutting in)* Oh, Katie — how could you do this to us

34

after all we've done for you? We've tried to bring you up decently. We sent you to the best schools —

FATHER: We're wasting time. She was always pig-headed!

Clock strikes three.

Fade down MOTHER and FATHER, who now go out.

MATT and KATE freeze; then, during the chimes, they move to opposite sides of the stage, from where they address the audience.

KATE: It's all going wrong. I knew it would.

MATT: Perhaps she's right. Perhaps I *am* bored. I'm restless — I know that.

KATE: It was all right before we married.

MATT: And yet I love her.

KATE: I know he loves me — but he ought to be free to love other women as well. You can't keep a poet in a cage — and that's what marriage is!

MATT: Was it a mistake to marry her?

KATE: You can't own another person. You can't have property rights on another person.

MATT: It used to be so good.

KATE: It was all right as long as we were lovers and were still free people.

MATT: What's gone wrong? Is it wrong to go out and have fun now and then?

KATE: I want to have fun too. Every night after work he's in the pub. It's like having a party every night!

MATT: It's good to relax over a jug of beer. Friends, good talk —

KATE: And women!

MATT: She's jealous of my friends.

KATE: Who wouldn't be in my position. They practically own him.

MATT: I give her plenty of sex.

KATE: When I want him most, he's either impotent with the booze or too tired. *(Bitterly)* But he's not too tired where other women are concerned.

MATT turns and addresses KATE for the first time.

MATT: What are you insinuating?

KATE: Oh, stop pretending! The other night —

MATT: What about it?

KATE: You came home smelling of another woman.

MATT: Bullshit!

KATE: Oh, yes you did! Too bad you forgot to wash! It's not like you to forget details like that. You must have been pissed to beat the band! Excuse the language! Matt — I want to be the 'other woman' for a change. I want to be your lover again. I don't want to be your wife any more.

KATE snatches off her ring and throws it at MATT's feet, then runs out.

MATT: Kate! *(Picks up the ring.)* Oh, hell! What a ballsup! I should never have married. I'm not the marrying type. I feel like chucking the whole thing up and clearing off —

SCENE TEN

Sudden cross-fade to WARNER standing in his position.

WARNER: With Sally? I hear you've been seeing her again.

MATT: *(Turns round, startled)* Perhaps. Nothing's been settled.

WARNER: What about Kate? What had you planned for her?

MATT: Planned? I hadn't got as far as planning. But it did occur to me that she might go back to her parents.

WARNER: *(Grunts)* Very convenient, I must say. Her parents don't want her any more than you do. That's part of her problem. She feels she's a burden that's better out of the way.

MATT: I haven't always felt like that about her, as you know. At the moment I'm confused. I don't know what to do.

WARNER: You're divided — and so is she. You'd be most unwise to make any decision while in this frame of mind. Matt, you must understand this. So far, Kate has done all the adjusting — and it's proved too much for her. She's made a terrific effort to fit in with you. She's adopted your life, your interests, your friends — and she's given up her own in doing so. Matt, if you decide your marriage is worth saving, you'll have to work much harder at it. You'll have to make a real effort to adjust more to her. I don't know if you're up to it — and in any case it may be too late.

MATT turns and addresses the audience.

COLIN enters unsteadily, with a bottle, and sits down in MATT's position. MATT is never aware of him.

MATT: Well — you heard the man. Not very encouraging, was he?

36

He's a good enough headshrinker, as headshrinkers go, but I doubt if he's ever twigged to my basic problem —

WARNER: *(As he goes out)* Don't you believe it!

MATT: *(Disconcerted)* Well — never mind that.

MATT walks to and fro, talking hesitantly, but with great sincerity.

COLIN's slurred interjections, most of them running behind MATT's speech, provide a kind of gloss to MATT's words.

The problem's this. I have no identity . . .

COLIN: Matt, you sad bastard — have a beer.

MATT: I lost it years ago when I denied my Maori blood . . .

COLIN: You had to do it. Matt. You had to run away from your old man.

MATT: I'm not a real Maori . . .

COLIN: Proper old bastard!

MATT: I don't act like one. I don't feel like one . . .

COLIN: Don't be ashamed of your heritage, boy.

MATT: Why did I deny the Maori in me?

COLIN: Be proud — hic — of heritage.

MATT: It was really my father I denied. I remember as a small boy trying to scrub my colour off. I wanted to be invisible.

COLIN: *(Quickly)* If you're invisible, they can't see your arse to kick it. Right, boy?

MATT: *(Ruefully)* I succeeded only too well. But that's a long story, and it's not really to the point . . .

COLIN: There's no point — that's the point!

MATT: I can't adjust, because there's nothing of me to adjust. Poor Kate's in love with a phantom . . .

COLIN: She's in love with *you.*

MATT: Do you know what I've been shopping round for in the desperate supermarket of other women's arms? An identity kit.

COLIN: Have a drink, Colin. Don't mind if I do. *(Takes a swig.)*

MATT: If I find it, perhaps Kate will at last have some one worthy of her love — and I shall recover my dignity as a human being . . .

COLIN: Good on you, Matt!

MATT: A Maori — and proud of it!

Laughter, off-stage, from KATE.

COLIN: Good on you! *(Staggers off.)*

KATE and GRANDFATHER enter.

KATE: What a killing wedding photo! But why was it taken in a glasshouse?

G'FATHER: A glasshouse? That's a conservatory. You were nobody if you didn't have a conservatory.

MATT: *(Raising his voice)* Meanwhile — in a very real sense — I'm as much a racist as Kate's grandfather over there. *(Points.)*

SCENE ELEVEN

Fade up KATE and her GRANDFATHER.

MATT goes across to join them.

KATE: This photograph has been torn out. All that's left is an eye, part of a nose and a mouth. It's a nice mouth — gentle, humorous. Who ripped it out?

G'FATHER: I did.

KATE: But why?

G'FATHER: He let the family down.

KATE: *(Amused)* What did he do? Rob old women? Rape little girls?

G'FATHER: *(Stiffly)* He was a conscientious objector — and don't be flippant, my dear. He spent most of the First World War in gaol.

KATE: He must have been a very brave man!

G'FATHER: Brave!

KATE: What became of him, Grandpa?

G'FATHER: As you'd expect, he went to the dogs. Ended up by marrying a Maori — some kind of princess I believe. Lots of piccaninnies running about — all that sort of thing.

KATE: Grandpa!

G'FATHER: Eh? Oh! *(Looks quickly at MATT and back at KATE.)* Terribly sorry, my dear. *(Turns away.)*

MATT: *(Taking KATE to one side)* Kate — if we don't get out of here soon, I'm going to start throwing the furniture about.

KATE: *(Startled)* We'll leave now. *(Handing GRANDFATHER the album)* I'm sorry, Grandpa — we have to go.

G'FATHER: Must you? But you've just arrived! Oh, well — if you must, you must.

KATE: Matt has a poetry reading. Oh, by the way, I brought you a copy of our wedding photograph — if you can call it that. *(Gives it to him.)*

G'FATHER: *(Barely looking at it)* Charming, my dear. I must add it to my collection. Tell me — where are you staying until you get a flat?

KATE: With Ralph. He offered to put us up.

G'FATHER: I see. And his wife — June — how is she?

KATE: She's in hospital, having a baby. Ralph is baching.

G'FATHER: *(Laughs drily)* He's always had women running after him. Won't do him any harm to look after himself for a change. *(Pausing, before going out, and looking MATT straight in the eye)* Pity you're not staying longer, sir. I'd like to have shown you my collection of dried heads.

MATT stares at him in astonishment, then bursts out laughing.

GRANDFATHER slowly and deliberately tears the photograph into pieces and walks off.

Fade down MATT, still laughing, and KATE, sitting slumped in the sofa.

SCENE TWELVE

Fade up MATT, as he comes forward to face the audience.

MATT: I had been painting the blue sky
a brighter blue.
I had been higher than I thought possible.
When I fell,
the sun wheeled spokes of light
about my head.

I make no excuses for my fall —
anyone that aims at such heights
must take the necessary precautions.
He must take care
to lean his ladder against a fixed object,
preferably a star.

O love, knowing your constancy,
how did I fail
to lean it against your heart?

(Turning to KATE) Do you like my poem? I wrote it for you.

KATE: I don't know if I understand it — but I do like it.

MATT: *(Going over to her)* How do you feel now?

39

KATE: Much better, darling. I'm sorry — I think Grandpa did upset me a little.

MATT: He's a monster.

KATE: Not really — he's just ignorant.

MATT: You can say that again.

KATE: Matt, you run along and have a good time. I'll be all right.

MATT: I hate poetry readings.

KATE: I know you do, but you mustn't disappoint your admirers.

MATT: Admirers — huh! I don't want to leave you alone in the house.

KATE: But Ralph's home.

MATT: Perhaps that's why I'm worried. He's tight.

KATE: What is it, Matt? Don't you trust me?

MATT: It's not that. It's — oh, I don't know. I just feel uneasy, that's all. It probably has nothing to do with Ralph at all. I mean — he can't help being a slob.

KATE: Matt, come here. *(Takes his hand.)* How can I convince you? I love *you*. The thought of another man's hands on me gives me the shudders.

MATT: I know all that. I'm sure you love me. It's just that . . . Oh, forget it.

KATE: You'd better go now — and hurry back.

MATT: Can I get you anything before I go?

KATE: No, darling. I have everything I need.

MATT: You look tired.

KATE: I'm very tired. I'll read awhile — then turn out the light. *(As MATT turns to go)* Matt?

MATT: Yes, Kate.

KATE: I'm sorry about the other night — the terrible thing I said.

MATT: *(Kisses her)* Bless you, love. I'd forgotten it. *(Reaches in his pocket.)* Oh, by the way, I think this belongs to you. *(Slips ring on her finger.)*

KATE: *(Moved)* Matt . . . Thank you.

MATT: Good night.

KATE: Good night, my darling.

MATT goes out.

SCENE THIRTEEN

Fade light to very dim, as MATT goes out.

Beam thin light directly on telephone, which is to the side.

KATE sits irresolutely, then hurries over and dials.

KATE: Hello ... is that Dr Warner? It's Kate Thompson. Kate Thompson. I used to be Kate James ... That's right ... Not very well ... That's why I'm ringing ... What? .. No, it's not that. My marriage is fine. It's me. I don't know quite how to tell you. It sounds silly when you put it into words ... That's the trouble — I don't know. One moment I'm perfectly all right, and the next, I — I feel panicky. It's as if the sky had suddenly darkened over. That doesn't make sense, I know. It doesn't last long as a rule, but while it's there I have the awful feeling of being trapped. I want to bang, bang, bang my head until I can't think any more. I'm like that now. I — I feel I must escape somewhere — anywhere. But there's nowhere to go — and without Matt I'd be unbearably lonely ... What? Matt? He doesn't know. I didn't want to worry him. He has had enough on his mind, poor darling! ... What? Oh, he thinks Mum and Dad and Grandpa are all ranged against him ... Grandpa is difficult, I agree ... I feel much better now. I think all I needed was a shoulder to cry on ... Thank you. Good night.

KATE looks more cheerful, as she hangs up.
Fade out telephone light, as she goes back to the sofa. Pause, as she sits there thinking, then the silence is broken by the sound of applause. (This can be produced by the off-stage actors.)

Fade up MATT, who takes up his position, looking ill at ease. A well-dressed CHAIRWOMAN, from MOTHER'S position, introduces him.

C'WOMAN: Thank you, thank you! And now the moment we've all been waiting for. Wellington's own homegrown poet — if I may call you that, Mr Thompson — will now entertain us with a reading of his poems. *(Claps.)* Ladies and gentlemen, Mr Matthew Thompson. *(Withdraws.)*

MATT: *(Nervously)* Thank you — um ... *(Coughs.)* I want you to hear a new poem I've been working on. It's called 'Purple Chaos'.

RALPH enters furtively during the first verse. He should be as much a menacing presence, as a man.

MATT: 'Chaos is purple.' you said.
'A painter's phrase,' I said,
disagreeing.

41

'Chaos is a colourless force
tossing up stars, flowers
and children,
and has no beginning
and no end.'

RALPH calls out in a loud whisper, unsettling both MATT and KATE at the same time.

RALPH: Kate!

KATE sits up inquiringly and MATT's memory suddenly fails him.

MATT: I'm sorry — I seem to have forgotten my lines. *(Takes a piece of paper from his pocket.)*
RALPH: Kate! *(Lurches towards her.)*
KATE: Who's that? *(Recognising him)* Oh, it's you!
MATT: I'll read the rest.

RALPH has to act quickly to have KATE, where he wants her, at the precise dramatic moment.

MATT's reading of the second verse should form a background to the violent movement and dialogue taking place in the main area, but, to be fully effective, the final verse should sound out clearly over the couple, who should then be still.

But lying in bed,
washed up,
I know you are right.
You were talking of something else —
you were talking of death.
Purple chaos has surged through me,
leaving me stranded —
a husk,
an empty shell,
on a long white swerving beach.
RALPH: Don't be afraid.
KATE: *(Sharply)* What do you want?
RALPH: I want *you* — I couldn't sleep.

He reaches for her and they struggle.

KATE: Let — me — go!
RALPH: Come on, Kate.
KATE: You're hurting me.

RALPH: Come on — be a sport!

KATE: What's got into you? Ralph, if you go now, I won't say a word to Matt.

RALPH lets her go in disgust.

RALPH: Bloody hell! Are you frigid or something?

KATE: I love Matt.

RALPH: Don't be so bloody wet!

KATE: You're disgusting!

RALPH grabs her again.

RALPH: Come on — we're wasting time.

He forces her back on to the sofa and, after a brief struggle, he holds her still.

Rooster crows.

MATT: Something has died,
    something precious has died.
    It may have been a flower,
    a star,
    it may have been a child —
    but whatever it was, my love,
    it seems to have died.

The clock strikes three.

During the chimes, MATT moves down to the main area and sees RALPH bent over KATE on the sofa.

(Furiously) What the hell's going on?

RALPH: (Springing apart) Take it easy, Matt — I can explain.

MATT: Get out, I'll deal with you later.

RALPH: Whose bloody house is this?

MATT: Get out!

RALPH glares at him, and as he leaves, spits out at him.

RALPH: Shit!

MATT: All right, Kate — what happened?

KATE: (Bursts into tears) Matt — I tried — I tried —

MATT looks at her wide, distraught eyes, and assumes the worst.

MATT: You slept with him. You rotten bitch — you whore! I knew I couldn't trust you. Christ — I'll kill you! I'll fucking well kill

43

you. *(Reaches for her throat.)*

KATE screams.

Black out.

SCENE FOURTEEN

SISTER is immediately on the scene. As the light flashes on, she is already reassuring KATE and leading her from the sofa to the chair.

KATE goes unwillingly.

SISTER: You're all right, Mrs Thompson. You were just having a bad dream. Come along now — that's the girl. *(As KATE sits down)* That's it. Now sit there, dear, while I get your pills. *(Goes out.)*

Fade up KATE, who is quite collected, as she addresses the audience.

KATE: Well, as you see, I'm still alive — Poor Matt! I warned you, didn't I? He's hopelessly insane. It's jealousy that's done it. He's always been madly jealous. I suppose it has to do with age, fear of competition from younger men, diminishing virility — not that he's shown any signs of that! He's still as sexy as a bantam rooster. *(Giggles.)* Anyway ... What was the point I was trying to make? *(Pause)* Oh yes — Matt's insane jealousy! It's finally tipped him over. He's madder than I am now — if such a thing is possible — which I doubt.

SISTER returns with glass of water and pills.

SISTER: Your pills, Mrs Thompson.

KATE washes pills down, then waves SISTER away.

KATE: One other thing — to put you in the picture. That tiresome exhibition of jealousy you saw took place seven months ago, and although we've gone over and over it together a thousand times since then Matt is still not convinced I didn't sleep with Ralph. Do you want him? He's yours.

SCENE FIFTEEN

Sudden cross-fade to WARNER.

KATE immediately raises her voice and speaks imperiously.

KATE: Doctor — I think you ought to know I'm no longer living with my husband. I had to send him away.

WARNER: Would you like to tell me what happened?

KATE: Gladly — but aren't you getting sick of my private circus. Well, a few nights ago, Matt came home very drunk and again brought up the subject of Ralph.

MATT, who is sitting in his position, speaks in a very slurred voice.

MATT: I think you slept with him.

KATE turns her head.

KATE: Matt, I've told you the truth —

MATT: Lies — bloody lies!

KATE: I did not sleep with him — and, if I did, what difference would it make?

WARNER: Oh, dear!

KATE: *(To WARNER)* I don't know what made me say that.

MATT is on his feet, swaying.

MATT: So you do admit sleeping with that bastard?

KATE: I admit nothing of the sort. You're drunk and disgusting — and I'm tired. *(To WARNER)* Then he began to shout.

MATT looms over her.

MATT: Admit it — go on, admit it. That baby's his, isn't it? *(Weaves over her in a threatening way, then slowly lurches out.)*

KATE: *(To MATT)* Perhaps. *(To WARNER)* I was fed up and wanted to hurt him. I thought he was going to attack me again. I screamed and ran out of the house. I went to Jill's place. She's our next-door neighbour.

WARNER: And then?

KATE: I rang the police. Then I asked some of the neighbours to go and keep an eye on Matt.

WARNER: Why did you do that?

KATE: I was sure he was dangerous and out to kill me — and besides the baby was still in the house. I knew Simon would be all

45

right — but there was no telling what Matt would do to Mary if he really believed she was Ralph's baby.

WARNER: Then what happened?

KATE: The police came — but by that time things had simmered down. They asked a few questions, but soon left. They could see it had just been a family row. They were very nice about it, considering. I suppose they get used to that sort of thing. Anyway — Matt and I had a good long talk. We even counted the months back to the time when I must have conceived — and Matt had to admit that Ralph couldn't possibly have been Mary's father. Still, after what had happened, I couldn't have him round the house, could I? I had to send him away.

WARNER: When did this happen, did you say?

KATE: Two or three nights ago.

WARNER: I see. How do you feel about him now? Do you want him back home?

KATE: I don't know, Doctor. What do you advise?

WARNER: That's up to you.

KATE: If you must know — I'm seriously thinking of asking him to come back home.

WARNER: I'm glad of that.

Slow fade, as KATE and WARNER go out.

SCENE SIXTEEN

Thin beam, as before, on the telephone.

MATT enters sleepily, after it has been ringing about ten times, and snatches up the receiver.

MATT: Yeah ... What? Oh, it's you. Hell of a time to ring, isn't it? *(Looks at watch.)* It's not six o'clock. ... What's it to you where I was last night? ... What? ... If you want to know — Colin and I went on the piss. That's why you couldn't get hold of me. ... Yeah, yeah — anyway, what do you want? ... Why the hell should I sound friendly? Look, Kate, think back. You kicked me out a few nights back. You had the whole neighbourhood convinced I was mad — and you said some pretty rough things to me — that I'm irresponsible, gutless, good-for-nothing — or have you forgotten? ... *I don't think it's funny.* ... What? You're asking me to come home! ... Of course I want to see Simon! ... Poor kid! ... All right, Kate — you

46

win . . . No, I don't need time to think about it. I'll come as soon as I can. I've a few things to do in town, then I'll come straight out . . . Goodbye.

As MATT puts down receiver, cry of gull causes him to look up, as if following its flight.

SCENE SEVENTEEN

Fade out telephone light and fade up main light to dim, as MATT walks slowly forwards and stops, centre, to speak his lines dejectedly.

MATT: Sickened by petrol fumes,
       stunned by grinding gears
       and the shouting of children
       laying siege to a school,
       I steady myself on a stone
       under a critical tree,
       high above the sea.

       My senses wince, ambushed
       by a sudden stench
       from weeds in a wet ditch.
       Tears fall on my hands —
       and I stare helplessly
       at an outcrop of rock
       unmoored by a choppy sea.

       I know nothing can be gained
       by staying here,
       confused by a wind
       glittering with knives —
       but, if I sit quite still
       and make my mind a blank,
       at least nothing too terrible
       can happen to me.

Cry of gull again, then the sound of KATE, off-stage, singing quietly 'Here we go gathering nuts in May'.

SCENE EIGHTEEN

Fade up main light to bright, as JILL enters and sees MATT.

JILL: Matt — thank God! I was afraid you wouldn't come.
MATT: Hello, Jill — what are you doing mixed up in this circus?
JILL: Holding the fort until you came.
MATT: It's like that, is it? Where is she?
JILL: In the bedroom, making herself pretty for you.
KATE: *(Off-stage)* Is that you, Matt?
MATT: Yes, Kate — it's me.
KATE: I won't be long.
MATT: How is she, Jill?

KATE enters, holding baby.

KATE: Matt?
JILL: Well — I'll leave you to it. *(Goes out.)*
MATT: What a pretty dress! Is it new? And your hair — I like it
        loose! What have you done to it? It seems to give off light.
KATE: *(Pleased)* I washed it, you idiot! Want to see the baby?
MATT: Very much.
KATE: *(Holds up baby)* Behold — the Sleeping Beauty! To wit:
        your supremely lovely daughter. *(Pause)* Well?

Moved, MATT tries to embrace her.

MATT: Kate! Oh, Kate —
KATE: *(Freeing herself)* Really, Matthew — stop pawing me. You
        must try to control yourself. And in front of your infant
        daughter, too. Whatever must she think?

KATE hums as she rubs the baby's back.

KATE: That's the good girl. There, there, poppet. *(Holds her up
        and studies her face.)* Oh, dear, I know a mother shouldn't have
        such thoughts, but sometimes I wish you weren't so dark.
MATT: She's beautiful.
KATE: Gorgeous — I know, I know! *(Resentfully)* But why can't
        people leave us alone? Sometimes I'm ashamed of being seen in
        the street with Mary. When I see the contemptuous looks other
        women give me, I want to wash her colour off.
MATT: May I hold her, dear?
KATE: *(Testily)* Not now, darling. Too many people holding her
        only upsets her. Isn't there something you can do?
MATT: *(Disconcerted)* But — Kate —

48

KATE: Oh, God — you men make me mad! You're so helpless. *(Shouts.)* Do anything! Don't stand there bug-eyed. A grown man ought to be able to amuse himself. *(Quieter)* You're giving the baby colic — isn't he, Mary baby? *(Sharply)* Now get the sulks and leave.

MATT: *(Coldly)* That's what I intend to do.

KATE: Can't you take a joke? *(As she leaves, with baby)* Honestly, you're more trouble than any child!

MATT stares after her angrily.
Pause, as he stands indecisively, then he comes forward and says his lines in a tired, disillusioned voice.

MATT: Your eyes don't know me.
Your body no longer says yes to me.
You have shifted house
taking your bits and pieces
from my mind.

So I've brought you something
in a small black box.
I think it's dead.
I'll put it on the table
beside the white flowers.

Goodbye — I'm going now.
I've gone out the door and shut it
carefully behind me.
The door . . . is . . . gone.

Long pause before KATE returns.

KATE: Well, I thought you were leaving.

MATT: I changed my mind.

KATE: You're as fickle as a woman . . . And how are your homosexual friends anyway? How are they all?

MATT: *(Taken aback)* What's eating you now, for Christ's sake, woman?

KATE: You know very well. *(Slily)* Your secret is out, you know. People are talking.

MATT: Let's get this straight. Have you been saying I'm a queer?

KATE: Yes, I have. *(Pause)* No, I won't say that. You might have me up for slander. *(Cautiously)* What I told them was that I suspected you of homosexual tendencies. *(Angrily)* What other reason have you for wanting me locked up in a mental home?

MATT: But I don't want you locked up.

KATE: Oh, yes you do. You want to shut my mouth. *(Bitterly)* Nobody believes a lunatic! Anyway, it's too late, Matthew Thompson. I've seen through you at last. *(Nastily) They're* looking into it now.

MATT: *(Shouts)* What are they looking into?

KATE: Try to control yourself. You were never one for self-control, were you? That's been half your trouble. You weren't brought up, you were dragged up — in a pa! You showed magnificent bravery and determination in pulling yourself out of the muck — but it's left its mark.

MATT: Look, Kate — I asked you a question. *Who* are looking into *what?*

KATE: I'm sure that's not the question you asked. But who am I to quibble? *Who* are looking into *what?* Is that the question? *(Matt nods angrily.)* Just people — friends of mine. That answers 'who'. Now Watt. *(Flippantly)* Watt is his name. Get it, Matty darling? *(Laughs.)* Stop gritting your teeth. You look like a villain in a Victorian melodrama.

MATT: *(Suspecting there is no such person)* Is he the lawyer you threatened me with the other night?

KATE: Right first time! He's going to confirm my suspicion you're a homosexual and publish it to the world.

MATT: And Dr Warner — does he know?

KATE: Naturally.

MATT: And your father — does he know?

KATE: But, of course! He was the first to know.

MATT: *(Amused)* Things couldn't be worse, could they?

KATE: *(Lightly)* You said it — not I!

MATT: Kate — let's restore some sanity to all this.

KATE: *(Coldly)* Some people round here have their own idea as to which of us is insane. Who was it tried to get rid of rats by pouring pepper down a rat-hole? Dr Warner is very concerned about you. But don't worry, my dear. They'll not lock you up — not if I can help.

KATE suddenly groans and puts her hands to her head.

MATT: What is it, Kate? *(Goes to help her.)*

KATE: *(Hysterically)* Keep away from me! Oh, my head! Where's Jill? *(Calls.)* Jill! *(Pushes MATT away.)* Don't touch me. I can sit down without any help from you. *(Sits down unsteadily on the sofa.)*

JILL enters, left, and puts her arm round KATE's shoulder.

JILL: It's all right, Kate.

KATE: *(Forlornly)* You won't leave me, will you, Jill? You'll stay with me?

JILL: Of course, I'll stay. You know that.

KATE: I need your protection. I might be locked up. Oh, oh — he'd do anything, Matthew would! Why do you want to put me into hospital, Matthew? *(Gently)* Matthew, sit down beside me — I won't bite you, silly!

MATT sits down.

Matt — if you really feel I have to go, I'll sign myself in without any help from you. *(Touches his wrist.)* Do you know what I mean? I'd have it on my conscience. *(Pleads.)* Matt — you're my husband! If I can't trust you, who can I trust?

MATT: Please believe me, Kate — I don't want to put you into hospital.

KATE: But you tried to once, didn't you?

MATT: That was your idea. You suggested a rest-home, but when we got there you changed your mind. Anyway, you're not so sick now.

KATE: *(Hardening)* So, you think I'm sick, do you?

MATT: Well, perhaps not sick — but I do think you're tense.

KATE: So you think I'm tense, do you? Well, let me tell you — I *am* tense. I hate you Matthew Thompson — that's what makes me tense.

JILL: *(Quickly)* Shall I make some tea, Kate?

KATE: *(Sweetly)* What a lovely idea, Jill. Matt and I have still some things to discuss — haven't we, dear?

MATT: Huh!

Silence as JILL leaves room.

MATT: Look, Kate — I've had enough. I can't take any more.

KATE: Why did you come then?

MATT: I came to talk things over, calmly and collectedly —

KATE: Aren't we doing just that? I'm sure I am. *(Hardens.)* But you find it difficult to be calm and collected, don't you?

MATT: Kate — lay off, or I'll leave.

KATE: You're a free agent. You can come and go as you please. It's a joint family home. I'm not forcing you to stay — and don't say I forced you to come! You came of your own free will.

MATT: But on the phone you seemed anxious to see me. You wanted me to catch the earliest train —

KATE: None of your lies. Think back. Can't you remember clearly?

Do you feel confused?

MATT: But, Kate —

KATE: I asked you to *think* about it and ring back — but you made up your mind at once. Think again, Maori boy. Things are going to be different round here from now on. You're not going to push me around any more. I won't stand for it. I'm not one of your children. I'm a responsible woman with a family to look after. If you're thinking of coming back, that's one thing I want you to be clear about. I'm sick — sick, do you hear? — of being pushed around. I refuse to be junior partner in this firm. Is that clear?

MATT: Yeah, ma'am.

KATE: You're a brilliant man, Matthew Thompson — but you're not the only one with brains. There are a lot of people just as clever as you. Remember that. And they're watching you very closely. I don't trust you an inch. I love you very much — but I don't trust you an inch. *(Pause)* Why don't you say something?

JILL returns with tray, on which are three mugs of tea, a jug of milk, a bowl of sugar and a teaspoon, and puts it on the sofa beside KATE.

KATE: How kind you are, Jill. *(Picks up milk jug.)* We all take milk, don't we?

MATT: And sugar.

KATE: I know that, you chump. That's one thing I've learnt in our brief marriage — perhaps the only memorable thing. When they come to write your biography I'll be able to tell them that Matthew Thompson, the great Maori bard, the Swan of Porirua, had sugar in his tea. *(As she puts in the sugar)* One and half tea-spoons — no more, no less.

KATE stirs quickly, then hands MATT his tea.

MATT: Very funny, I'm sure. *(Sips.)* Well, there's still one thing to decide.

KATE: What's that?

MATT: Simon's future.

KATE: That's your problem. I'm only the wicked stepmother. What about his mother? Can't she take him? Jill?

JILL: Yes?

KATE: Did you know I'm not legally responsible for Simon? Matthew, dear trusting Matthew, didn't get round to filing the adoption papers. A fine, trusting husband you turned out to be! Did you know Simon is terrified of you? Well, he is! And as for your precious love — I'm not taken in by it. It's a terrible possessiveness — an evil thing! *(Wearily)* Well — you're his father. Make up your own mind. I can't make it up for you.

MATT: I've made up my mind.

KATE: *(Suddenly vulnerable)* What — what are you going to do?

MATT: I'm taking him back to town with me.

KATE gasps.

JILL: But, Matt!

MATT: If we're going to separate — Simon comes with me.

KATE: Who's talking of a separation?

MATT: You have — often. I never took you seriously before, but now I do. So — Simon comes with me.

KATE jumps wildly to her feet.

KATE: I'd better ring Daddy.

JILL: No — don't do that.

KATE: I'll ring Dr Warner. *(Rushes out.)*

MATT looks at JILL.

MATT: All right — say it.

JILL: If you were to go now, taking Simon —

MATT: Go on.

JILL: She'd be lost. She desperately wants you to stay.

MATT: Funny way she has of showing it!

JILL: Take no notice of what she says. It's her way of telling you she's in trouble and needs your help. Matt — if you've ever felt any love for her — please, please stay!

MATT: You know — in spite of everything that's happened I'm in love with her. Crazy, isn't it? Of course I'll stay.

JILL: But try not to argue with her. Agree with everything she says. Oh, it'll be tough — but it may work.

KATE enters triumphantly.

KATE: Dr Warner's on the phone. He wants to speak to you, Matt.

MATT puts his mug on the tray and walks across to the telephone, while KATE returns to the sofa, where JILL stands protectively beside her.

Fade in WARNER in position.

SCENE NINETEEN

MATT picks up the receiver.

MATT: Yes?

WARNER: Well, frankly, Matt — I don't like the sound of things. She's a sick girl. Hasn't made the progress I'd hoped for. You seem to be having a rough time. How are you taking it?

MATT: I'm surviving.

WARNER chuckles.

What are we going to do?

WARNER: We'll wait another twenty-four hours. If you see further signs of deterioration, let me know.

MATT: Right.

WARNER: What have you decided about Simon?

MATT: What did she tell you?

WARNER: As much as I needed to know.

MATT: He's staying.

WARNER: Good, good. And you?

MATT: I'm staying, too.

WARNER: That's fine. Have you sleeping pills?

MATT: I think so.

WARNER: Take a couple tonight. Try to get Kate to take them, too.

MATT: Not much chance of that. She's even given up tranquillisers!

WARNER: They might undermine her self-control, eh?

MATT: Yes — she's hanging on like grim death.

WARNER: *(Chuckles.)* She has spirit, that girl. Well, I'm afraid you're in for a pretty rough night. Better batten down hatches and try to ride out the storm.

MATT puts down receiver.

Fade out WARNER.

SCENE TWENTY

As MATT puts down the receiver, KATE turns to JILL and speaks.

KATE: This is Simon's home. It would be wrong to take him away.

MATT returns.

MATT: Kate?

KATE: Yes, Matt.

MATT: Simon is staying. I'd like to stay, too — may I?

KATE: If you like. I'm not forcing you, but you'll make Simon very happy, if you do stay.

MATT: And you, Kate — how about you?

KATE: Me? Why — of course, I want you to say. You don't know how much I love you. *(Tearful)* You're everything to me. I love you. Nothing makes sense without you.

JILL: *(Very practical)* Why don't you two run out and sit on the cliff? It's really lovely now. I'll get the tea started.

MATT: That's a great idea. How about it, Kate?

KATE: *(Suddenly worried)* Where's Simon — oh, where is he?

JILL: He's with a friend. He's all right. You run along.

KATE: I do wish he wouldn't wander off. It's a terrible responsibility being a stepmother.

MATT: Coming, Kate?

KATE: Not just now, dear. I'm much too busy. There's so much to do. The house is so untidy! But you go on. I'll join you later. *(Despairingly)* Everything's in such a mess. So much to do and so little time . . . so little time . . .

Fade down KATE and JILL, as MATT comes forward into a front light.

SCENE TWENTY-ONE

MATT speaks his lines quietly and with strong feeling.

MATT: Why do I post my love letters
in a hollow log?
Why put my lips to a knothole in a tree
and whisper your name?

The spiders spread their nets
and catch the sun,
and by my foot in the dry grass
ants rebuild a broken city.
Butterflies pair in the wind,
and the yellow bee,
his holsters packed with bread,
rides the blue air like a drunken cowboy.

More and more I find myself

talking to the sea.
I am alone with my footsteps.
I watch the tide recede
and I am left with miles of shining sand.
Why don't you talk to me?

As MATT is speaking his lines, KATE comes forward, so that she is now beside him.

KATE: Matt — that poem was about us, wasn't it?

MATT: Kate! Hello, darling. How are you feeling?

KATE: We just don't get through to each other, do we? We just don't communicate — we never have. *(Sits in her chair.)*

SISTER: *(Calling out)* Time's running out, Mr Thompson.

MATT: You're shivering! Why didn't you put on a cardigan?

KATE: I couldn't wait. I had to tell you before it's too late. There isn't much time.

MATT: What is it, Kate?

KATE: It's — Mary.

MATT: *(Alarmed)* Nothing's happened to her, has it?

KATE: *(Gently)* Nothing could happen to her. *They* are looking after her.

MATT: They? Who are they?

KATE: *(Laughs gently)* You'd really think I was mad if I told you. Trust me. That's all I ask. Mary is in good hands. *(Dreamily)* I know now why I was brought into this world. It was to give birth to — Mary. Have you noticed her hands — have you? They unfold like lotus petals — just like lotus petals. She's a creature apart. Matthew — are you listening? I've fulfilled my purpose. There's nothing left for me to do.

MATT: *(Gently)* You could look after her — and Simon.

KATE: Yes — but I'm so tired — so tired. *(Pause)* Matthew?

MATT: Yes, my love.

KATE: Look after my children when I'm gone. Promise me. They're so helpless — and yet so wonderful. Look at Mary. She can't do a thing for herself, but she's full of trust. She knows I will feed her and clothe her and take care of her. .... Children are so trusting — they trust you. .... It's a very great honour. *(Pause)* Matthew?

MATT: I'm listening.

KATE: We mustn't ever quarrel. It takes too much out of us. We Thompsons must stick together. We mustn't let anybody come between us — and we mustn't let people push us into mental homes. We must stand up for ourselves and have confidence and faith. . . . Promise me something.

MATT: What do you want me to promise?

KATE: That you won't do anything foolish.

MATT: Like what?

KATE: Like — taking your life.

MATT: I promise.

KATE: And promise me one more thing.

MATT: Anything.

KATE: Promise me you'll stop running away. You have to stop and face up to things, no matter how unpleasant. You can't run away from yourself, Matthew.

MATT: I'll try not to.

KATE: You must promise.

MATT: All right — I promise.

KATE shivers violently.

KATE: They're wrong when they say hell is hot. It's cold — freezing cold. *(Desolated)* I'm in hell, Matt. *(Long pause)* I've been waiting three nights . . .

MATT: What for?

KATE: I don't know — but I'm waiting . . .

Clock strikes three.

During the chimes, MATT slowly withdraws and takes up his position in line with the SISTER and WARNER, who should already be in position.

SCENE TWENTY-TWO

With the third chime, KATE comes out of a trance.

KATE: *(Anxiously)* Matt — where are you, darling? Matt? *(Listens.)* Matt? *(Desolate)* He's gone. It's all over. I've lost everything — husband, children . . . my mind. Everything's gone wrong. It's always been like that as long as I can remember . . .

Slight pause.

SISTER: *(Calling out)* Are you all right, Mrs Thompson?

FADE OUT

The Wide Open Cage

James K. Baxter, who died in 1972, was an extremely energetic writer: as well as his huge output of poetry, he wrote twenty-two plays and an unpublished novel. His dramatic writing came mainly in spasmodic bursts with the encouragement of directors like Richard Campion and Patric Carey; most of his plays seem relatively unpolished, and in places suggest a rather insecure sense of theatre. *The Wide Open Cage* was his first stage play, and it originally consisted only of Acts I and III — Act II was written at Richard Campion's suggestion. Its première (Unity Theatre, November 1959) was a sensational success, and it had a season Off-Broadway in 1962; some American critics were lavish in their praise, and it appealed particularly to Richard Sharp of *The Village Voice,* who found the language 'appropriately poetic and obscene and blasphemous.'

Several critics have observed that *The Wide Open Cage* is a contemporary passion play, and there is something of the Jacobean revenge tragedy about it, too. But basically it is a 'drop-out' drama, a play about people who have drifted outside normal social decencies, and the result is gut-level action and an attempt to probe fundamental human values. Baxter returned to his alcoholic sub-culture again and again in his plays; dramatically, he found the drunks an extremely expressive mirror to the whole chaotic Western World, as he saw it. In a radio talk, 'Some Possibilities for New Zealand Drama,' Baxter later confessed that he allowed his own opinions on the relationship of God to man to be expressed through the character of Father Tom, and he thought this a defect. In revivals of this play since Baxter's death, people have commented that Skully seems very close to Baxter, too, and it's perhaps worth pointing out that at the start of the second act Skully sees Hogan as being part of himself. The figures in Baxter's plays are not really 'characters' in the conventional naturalistic sense: once one gets past the superficial differentiation between them, they all seem like facets of a single person — they are all poets, they are all concerned with the same problems, and they all speak with Baxter's voice. Their power comes not from skills of objective dramaturgy but simply because the ego behind them was such a fascinating, many-sided thing.

In his 'Programme Note' to the first production Baxter wrote: This play has no message. It simply holds up a mirror to certain relationships among people. The Wide Open Cage is life itself; or, if you like, the inordinate love of creatures. The people in the play are each in their different ways trying to find happiness in other people; except for the priest, who is out of the running, and Hogan, who loves nobody. The fact that three of the people are catholics is really incidental. Catholicism brings to a head certain problems of freedom and involvement which are latent in all human relationships. To those inside the cage release seems to be the death of love.

Baxter's other principal plays are: *Jack Winter's Dream* (written 1956), *Three Women and the Sea* (1961), *The Spots on the Leopard* (1962), *Mr Brandywine Chooses a Gravestone* (1966), *The Band Rotunda, The Sore-footed Man, The Bureaucrat, The Devil and Mr Mulcahy* (all 1967), *Mr O'Dwyer's Dancing Party, The Day Flanagan Died* (both 1968), and *The Temptations of Oedipus* (1969).

CRITICAL ARTICLES on *The Wide Open Cage*

BERTRAM, JAMES 'The Wide Open Cage'. *Landfall* XIV, (1960), 81-4.

McNAUGHTON, HOWARD. 'Baxter as Dramatist'. *Islands* II, (1973), 184-92.

MASON, BRUCE. 'The Wide Open Cage'. *New Zealand Theatre* 112, (1959), 11-13.

POCOCK, J.G.A. A review of 'Two Plays: The Wide Open Cage and Jack Winter's Dream'. *Landfall* XIV, (1960), 197-201.

JAMES K. BAXTER

The Wide Open Cage

Characters

> JACK SKULLY, *a pensioner in his fifties*
> FATHER TOM O'SHEA, *a Redemptorist priest*
> NORAH VANE, *a woman in her late twenties*
> MRS BAILEY, *landlady to Skully*
> BEN HOGAN, *a drunk*
> TED HARDWICK, *a lad of eighteen*
> EILA, *a girl of seventeen*
> VOICE, *from skull*

SKULLY's two-room shack. Bedroom and living room are open to audience, but divided from each other by wall and door. A shelf of books: a skull on the shelf serving as bookrest. SKULLY and FATHER TOM playing euchre at a small table. NORAH lies on the bed smoking and reading magazines. She is dressed in trousers and a black sweater. SKULLY and the audience know of her presence; FATHER TOM does not.

SKULLY: There's an ace.

FR. TOM: There's a trump to beat it.

SKULLY: You're an old sly dog. If you weren't a priest, I'd say you'd kept that one up your sleeve.

FR. TOM: No, it's just the luck of the game.

SKULLY: As the sailor said when he found a woman in his bunk. Well, there's the right bower. You can't trump that one, Tom.

FR. TOM: It's yours, Skully. You've won the trick.

SKULLY: *(Begins to fold the pack)* Ah, what's the use! If we'd been playing for money, there might be something in it. Four pound ten a week. It's enough to buy tobacco, and that's all. I was making fifteen in the public works camp. Then the doctor laid me off. No lifting weights, he said. No undue excitement. A man might as well be a canary in a cage.

FR. TOM: You can't break the door down, Skully. It's the will of the Almighty. We're each of us in a cage till Judgement Day. Then God Himself will open the door for us.

SKULLY: Ah, put a sock in it, Tom! Your God and mine are two different things. Mine's not a prison governor. I can be honest with Him. He knows Jack Skully to the backbone. And when I put a foot wrong, I don't need a priest to make it up between us.

FR. TOM: Easy, man. No one ever said that God can't work outside the sacraments.

SKULLY: It's the churches that put men in a cage. Here's Jack Skully, heart, mind, bones, blood, arse and ballocks. What do the churches say to him? Climb into your coffin, they say. Lie down. It's lined with velvet and the water won't get inside. We'll say a prayer for the good of your soul. Maybe I don't want a prayer. Maybe I want a day at the races, with twenty quid in the kick, with the horses lively in the boxes and the balloon going up. Maybe I want a woman to wrap herself round me and keep the frost away. Maybe I want to live a bit before they shovel the sods over me.

FR. TOM: *(Gently)* Well, there's no harm in a bet, Skully. Riley told me on Wednesday: 'Stormy Petrel in the first leg of the double.' For the second leg, I fancy Rose of Kildare myself. It'll be a thumping divvy. If they both come in.

NORAH rises in the bedroom, moves about, knocks over an ashtray. She begins her toilet: hair and lipstick. She has difficulty with a gold comb; one to be worn as an ornament.

FR. TOM: What's that noise?

SKULLY: Ah, it'll be the rats, Tom. They come out in the daytime even. There was one came out three days ago, bold as brass, and sat in the middle of the floor. A grandfather rat, fatter than a priest. I could see his old grey whiskers. I hit him with the shovel. He was that long from tail to head. *(Indicates length of rat with his hands.)*

FR. TOM: It sounded more like someone walking about.

SKULLY: It's rats, nothing but rats. Don't try to change the subject. There's no harm in a bet, eh, Tom? But what about a woman? A woman in bed. A woman, Tom, with red ringlets on the pillow. You'd like me to call you Father, wouldn't you, Tom? Father This and Father That. 'Father, I'm sick, say a prayer for me, would you?' But it's Tom O'Shea I fought with at school, and he was no father. Call no man father, that's what the Bible says.

FR. TOM: Call no man good: that's the way I remember it. You can call me Bing Crosby, for all I care. If you need a woman, why don't you get married? Mrs Bailey would marry you tomorrow if you'd only ask. I've seen the look in her eye when she sews a button on your coat. A good Christian woman. Broadminded.

SKULLY: Broad as the gates of Hades. I'd never be able to talk or think. I'd be sitting like an old collie in a kennel under a tree. He can hear the shepherd whistle, but no one comes to unbuckle his collar.

FR. TOM: *(Rising, walking about)* It's a fine skull you've got there.

SKULLY: It's a mascot. A Maori head I dug out of a bog. In the sandhills east of Dannevirke.

FR. TOM: **Timor mortis conturbat me.** The fear of death stirs me up like a spoon.

SKULLY: Not me. Maybe you, with gold in the churches, gold on the altar, and a full collection —

FR. TOM: We get five shillings a week. Tobacco money. The gold belongs to God.

SKULLY: The God I know doesn't need a gold frame. He doesn't need a priest to make His meaning clear. *(He stands and begins unconsciously to re-enact the scene of his conversion.)* I sailed the Coast for thirty years, Tom. The *Kowhai* and the *Ocean Queen.* The only God I had came out of a bottle. Bloodhouses, jails, and a broken nose! That's what the bottle taught me. Well, I came to the end of that road outside a pub in Port Chalmers. Flanagan owned it. He shoved me out with nothing but the clothes I stood in. I hadn't eaten for eighteen days. I could feel the horrors coming on —

FR. TOM: Easy now, easy now!

SKULLY: I was damned already. 'Skully,' I said, 'you're in the breakers now.' A john was standing at the other side of the street. He wouldn't run me in. I taught him how to wrestle when he was a kid. Well, I dropped down on my benders *(he kneels on the stage)* and I called out — 'God', I said, 'If there is a God, help Jack Skully!' And God came down to me kneeling in the mud. He didn't need a priest — *(SKULLY rises)*

FR. TOM: I believe it, man. I know you've never touched a drop since. Maybe I could do with the same treatment. But a priest has to plod along from day to day. Once I wanted to be a sheep farmer and drive to the races in a big car. With a good Catholic wife and ten young O'Sheas. But Almighty God wanted another Redemptorist. He got His way in the end. *(He and SKULLY sit.)* Tell me, Skully, have you seen Hogan? Ben Hogan. He came out of Mount Crawford on Monday.

SKULLY: Mother Crawford's boarding house! Yes, I've seen Hogan. He was round here yesterday with a bottle of meths. Drunk as a pig. He was talking about burning down the house of the Beak that gave him six months. You'll never get Hogan to your Mission —

FR. TOM: It's not in your hands or mine.

SKULLY: Maybe. Who's kidding who, Tom? You're not here to find Hogan. Or to pick the double. Or to teach Jack Skully how to say his prayers. You're here to find Norah. Norah Vane. Does the name ring a bell? *(NORAH listens, finishes her toilet, comes to the door and leans down listening.)*

FR. TOM: It does.

SKULLY: You'll find her in the next room.

FR. TOM: I'll wait then.

SKULLY: She turned up last night without a bean. There's no boats in port.

FR. TOM: You gave her a bed. And she tempted you?

SKULLY: She didn't tempt me. I tempted her. With a bottle of sherry and a pound note.

FR. TOM: *(Groaning)* Are you glad about it?

SKULLY: No.

FR. TOM: Here she comes. *(Enter NORAH, goes to window, ignoring FATHER TOM.)*

NORAH: I see we've got visitors, Skully. There's blackbirds in the garden.

FR. TOM: Good day, Norah.

NORAH: *(Turning in mock surprise)* Oh, it's Father O'Shea. Good day, Father. It's a fine, bright morning. I expect you've got a lot of work on your hands. Keeping the choir in order. Making sure the women have babies. I'd rather not have ány myself.

SKULLY: Norah —

NORAH: You shut your stupid mouth. This is between me and the man in the black suit. *(To FATHER TOM)* I suppose you want to see me at the Mission, Father. I'm afraid I just won't have the time. *(Savagely)* You can put the Mission right up your arse. *(SKULLY stands up, moves nearer to her.)*

FR. TOM: *(Gently)* The Mission is God's work, not mine. There's no face I'd rather see there than your own. But it would be wrong to come to please me. Don't be angry, child. There's nothing to be afraid of. I'm just an old man talking. But you're a Catholic born and bred — it's in the blood. Suffering. The right kind or the wrong kind of suffering.

NORAH: I don't think you understand me, Father. It's all a matter of finding the right vocation. The nuns always told us to pray hard, and we'd find the right one. You've got a priest's vocation — to be a human blackbird, whistling on the branch, pecking for souls. I've got a vocation too. To be a kind of human gumboot. Don't think I'm mean about it, they always get more than they pay for. Skully darling — *(She goes to SKULLY and embraces him closely)* Give me another quid. I'll need it today to get started. *(SKULLY silently hands her a pound note. She turns again to face FATHER TOM.)*

Hunger, dark, and cold: the three ugly sisters. They stand above the cradle; they go to bed with every human soul; they hammer down the coffin lid. Where do you think the poor man finds his Heaven? Here! *(she presses her breasts)* Here! *(she presses her womb)* It's the nearest to easy dying they can get. *(She raises her voice)* Don't talk to me of Hell. Hell's being on your own. I've seen the time I'd talk to a fly on the rim of a whisky glass. And what was the Church doing? Saying: Repent for your sins. An old man like this one *(points to SKULLY)* has

65

got more pity in his little finger.

FR. TOM: You're right. Right and wrong. There's not enough love in the world we've made. God had to suffer alone in the Garden, and only an angel came to comfort Him. *(Rising)* I'll be here on Monday at nine o'clock, if you want to talk to me alone. God bless you. *(He makes the sign of the cross)* Take care of her Skully. *(Puts on his hat and goes.)*

NORAH: Give me a kiss, Skully. I want to smother the taste of holy water. *(They embrace.)* Ah, you may be an old man, Skully, but you're clean inside. I'd rather sleep with you than with a maharajah. *(She draws away suddenly.)* Who's that coming?

VOICE: Mr Skully! Mr Skully!

SKULLY: It'll be Ma Bailey. Get back inside the room.

NORAH returns to bedroom, kicks off her shoes, sits on the bed, reads, smokes.

VOICE: Mr Skully! Mr Skully!

SKULLY settles down in chair with the Sports Post, *puts on glasses.*

MA BAILEY: *(At the door)* Mr Skully! Are you deaf or something! I've been shouting all the way up the garden.

SKULLY: *(Takes off spectacles, folds paper)* Oh, it's you, Ma! What's the matter? You should save your breath for blowing up the chimney. Are the johns after me? You'd think they'd leave a man to die in peace. It can't be the rent. I paid you yesterday.

MA BAILEY: Don't joke about the police, Mr Skully. Not with the kind of friends you have here. That dreadful Hogan. Staggering over the flower beds. He broke down three of my best hydrangeas.

SKULLY: He's a sick man, Ma.

MA BAILEY: Sick or drunk. At least you leave the drink alone.

SKULLY: Meaning what?

MA BAILEY: There's other things besides drink.

SKULLY: A game of cards. A few bob on the horses. I need a couple of vices to pay the undertaker.

MA BAILEY: You don't play cards with that Maori girl. At your age you should be past it. *(She comes nearer the table, leans on it.)*

SKULLY: She's just a good friend, Ma. The old heart wouldn't stand for fun and games. You're my real girlfriend — aren't you? I like a woman with a bit of meat on her bones. *(He pats her behind. She bridles.)*

MA BAILEY: Don't be awful, Mr Skully. Anyone listening would think you meant it. Ah, there's a button off your coat. *(She picks it up from the floor and looks at it.)* If it wasn't for me you'd be going round in rags. *(She touches the sleeve of his coat.)* And the sleeves worn out. Leave it at the house and I'll mend it for you.

SKULLY stands up, takes off his coat, hangs it over a chairback, sits again.

SKULLY: I might get a new suit. Tom O'Shea told me the winner for the big race.

MA BAILEY: What is it?

SKULLY: Stormy Petrel.

MA BAILEY: Petrol? Petrol? That's a queer name for a horse.

SKULLY: Not the petrol that comes in a tin. It's a little grey and black bird. I've seen them running in front of a storm, a hundred miles from the coast of Peru. Skimming up and down the waves. Waves like pyramids. They'd scare a man, but not the little birds. They're at home in the storm.

MA BAILEY: Ah Mr Skully, you're like one yourself. It's not right for a man to live like you do — with only sluts and thieves for company.

SKULLY: Maybe they'll get to Heaven before I do, Ma.

MA BAILEY: You're not in Heaven yet. Why don't you settle down with a woman of your own age?

SKULLY: That's a hard one to answer. Maybe it's easier to play the horses than please a wife. How did your own marriage go? Did you like it?

MA BAILEY: A woman's got to be of use to someone. Mr Bailey was a great one for the horses too. He'd lose fifty pounds and never turn a hair. And he needed a lot of loving. A little scrawny man with a big nose, he was. Night and morning he had to have a bit of loving. Sometimes in the middle of the afternoon, when I was putting a roast in the oven, he'd touch me and say — 'Annie, I'm dying for it.' And I'd have to take my apron off and leave the roast alone. I'd never be nasty though. What use is a marriage if you can't keep your husband happy? When Mr Bailey passed away, life wasn't the same. I felt like a poor old car left to rust in a garage. Sometimes I wake up at night and find I'm stroking the hot water bottle. A woman's got to be of use, Mr Skully. Otherwise we're like the apple left on the end of the branch. ·

SKULLY: Why don't you come up and see me when you're lonely, Ma?

MA BAILEY: You never asked me, Mr Skully.

He puts his arm round her waist: she standing: he sitting.
Pause, then takes his arm away again.

SKULLY: You'd want me to toe the line too much. There's someone wild in here *(touches his chest)* who can't bear a locked door. Young Jack Skully, mad as a maggot, singing out in the dark. You're a fine woman, Ma, but we'd never make a go of it.

MA BAILEY: Ah, you're a hard man to please. *(She picks up the coat and puts it over her arm.)* I'll take this down to the house with me. *(She goes in silence to the door, then turns.)* I forgot to tell you. There's a young man asking for you. I'll send him up. But don't lend him any money. They all know you're an easy man to borrow from. *(She goes out the door, puts her head back in.)* What was the name of that horse? Petrel. Petrel. I'll put ten shillings on it myself. *(She goes out.)*

SKULLY settles down again: switches on the radio. Low music.
NORAH puts her head out the bedroom door, steps back into room.

NORAH: She's gone, eh? What an old bag!

SKULLY: There's nothing wrong with Ma. Maybe she's a bit inclined to natter. But there's many a good tune played on an old fiddle.

NORAH: You like her better than me.

SKULLY: Don't be Uncle Willy. You're my starlight, Norah. You're sweet poison. You're an old man's darling. *(They embrace.)*

NORAH: Get me a glass of sherry. *(SKULLY gets the bottle and pours. She drinks it. She takes his hand, looks at it, then bites him on the wrist.)*

SKULLY: Hey! What the hell did you do that for?

NORAH: There. I've put a mark on you. You belong to me now.
Steps outside. Door opens, and TED comes in.

SKULLY: Good day, Mr Hardwick. It's nice of you to pay me a visit. Welcome to Skully Castle. Is it money or a woman you want?

TED is silent and embarrassed.

NORAH: Excuse me. I'll have to go now. I told Ben Hogan I'd meet him before half-past ten. Excuse me. *(She goes into bedroom, emerges with handbag.)* Goodbye, Skully. I'll be back tonight. Don't forget me, husband.

She goes out door, ignoring TED. TED and SKULLY settle down.

TED: That's a finelooking girl.

SKULLY: Hands off! She's ecclesiastical property.

TED: How do you mean?

SKULLY: I'm keeping an eye on her for an old white-collared gentleman. And for my own bishopric. A blind eye in a bald head.

TED: You're luckier than I am. *(Head into hands, pause, then up.)* I can't stand it at home, Skully! There's no place to read or think. No one alive to talk to. My brother's got his Scout emblems on the wall. Mum thinks of nothing but clothes and cooking. My sister talks about the people in her office. *(Mimics)* 'A married man. Oh, mother, it's disgusting! He's running around with Florence Baker.' I don't know why she doesn't get hold of a man herself. It would take her mind off other people. And Dad's the worst of all —

SKULLY: What does he do?

TED: He sits by the fire and reads M.R.A. booklets. And he keeps on — farting.

SKULLY: Loud or soft?

TED: Very soft. But a terrible smell. Like the gasworks. I think he must be going rotten inside.

SKULLY: Well, it's only human nature. I can fart myself when I'm in the mood. After a feed of liver and onions.

TED: It's the way he does it, though. As if somebody else was to blame.

SKULLY: I know. There's a sanctimonious way of farting.

TED: You're a great standby, Skully. If it wasn't for you, I think I'd be going insane. *(He gets up, walks to bookcase, pulls out book, opens it)* What's this book?

SKULLY: Just poems. Read me something, Ted.

TED: Stark in the pasture on the skull-shaped hill,
In swollen aura of disaster shrunken and
Unsheltered by the ruin of the sky,
Intensely concentrated in themselves the banded
Saints abandoned kneel . . .

That's queer. I didn't know you read religious books.

SKULLY: There's a lot you don't know. But I like the sound of you reading it. Go on. Read the rest of it.

TED: And under the unburdened tree

Great in their midst, the rigid folds
Of a blue cloak upholding as a text
Her grief-scrawled face for the ensuing world to read,
The Mother, whose dead Son's dear head
Weighs like a precious blood-encrusted stone
On her unfathomable breast . . .

What's it all about, Skully?

SKULLY: Christ coming down from His Cross. It happens every day.

TED: I've never seen it happen.

SKULLY: Maybe your eyes aren't sharp enough. Read the bit that follows. *(TED hesitates.)* Here, give the book to me. *(Takes and reads.)*

SKULLY: Out of these depths:

Where footsteps wander in the marsh of death and an
Intense infernal glare is on our faces facing down:

Out of these depths, what shamefaced cry
Half choked in the dry throat, as though a stone
Were our confounded tongue, can ever rise:
Because the mind has been struck blind
And may no more conceive
Thy Throne . . .

That's where the spade strikes the granite. Do you know what it's like to be in Hell, Ted?

TED: I don't know. I might be there now.

SKULLY: It's the place beyond human help. A suffering that never ends. It's the lock-up where a proud man meets God face to face. Until you've been there, life is a dream — a thing of ambitions and fears and hopes. After you've been there, there's no hope left. No natural hope. Only the eyes of God burning a hole in your heart. A man can begin to rejoice.

TED: I'd like to find an easier road.

SKULLY: Go back then and kiss your old man's arse. Get a job selling douches. 'Guaranteed Sputnik Model. Try it out, madam. Rainbow coloured plastic. Brigitte Bardot uses one.'

TED: I could use Brigitte Bardot.

SKULLY: I'll bet you could. Listen to this now. *(Turns up radio.)*

RADIO VOICE: *(Singing)*

They was making mad . . . passionate love,
   Mad . . . passionate love,

When the lightning flashed and the thunder crashed
So the two little birdies flew away,
So the two little birdies flew away . . .
(cluck-cluck-cluck of birds) Ahh . . . Ahh . . . Ahh . . .

SKULLY: That's you and Brigitte Bardot. Humping in the park.

TED: It's no joke. You're all right. You're got women coming and going every day of the week.

SKULLY: Not so simple. They go more often than they come. Here, have some tea. It's well brewed — as black as tar. *(He pours tea.)*

TED: What's the name of that one? The woman that went out.

SKULLY: Norah. Norah Vane.

TED: I'd like to see her again. She looks lively enough. *(Raises voice.)* Oh, it's terrible, Skully. Trying to get hold of a woman. Day and night — but it's twice as bad at night. I went and had a yarn to the parson about it. He didn't say much. Just looked at me with that fish eye they've all got, and told me to keep my mind on higher things.

SKULLY: I had my first hump in a cattle truck. When I was fourteen.

TED: What was it like, Skully?

SKULLY: No bloody good. It was over in two minutes. The boys behind me in the line were shouting out for me to get a move on.

TED: Yesterday I went down to the skating rink and tried to pick up a sheila. There was one brunette. About eighteen. She grinned at me twice. But when I tried to talk to her, her boyfriend muscled in. I thought he was going to sock me. So I went out and walked along the wharves. A cold, white moon like a leghorn pullet, sitting on top of Mount Victoria. It wasn't hatching any eggs.

SKULLY: So you went home and laid an egg all on your own.

TED: How did you know? It's a terrible thing to do. My old man reckons, if you do that, sooner or later you go up the line.

SKULLY: If your old man was right, every man in the country would be locked in the giggle house. How do you think I get on when the duck shooting season's over? Read a book and sing myself to sleep? It's a pity you're not a Catholic, Ted. 'Father, I've committed a sin of impurity.' 'Who with, my son?' 'With myself, Father. I banged the bishop three times on Friday.' 'Say ten Our Fathers and ten Hail Marys. And go and find yourself a good Catholic girl.' You've got the wrong approach. You're not to blame for being born human.

71

TED: It helps a lot to hear you say it.

SKULLY: There's two kinds of people. Honest men and hypocrites. Maybe not conscious hypocrites. But the unconscious hypocrite is the world's worst killer. He looks in the mirror and sees Jesus Christ looking back at him. And then he goes out and tells the world to stop drinking, stop humping, stop laughing, stop frying spuds, and follow him. To the cemetery.

TED: How does a man become honest?

SKULLY: Don't ask me. I'm still learning. Look out the window instead. *(TED rises and looks out window.)*

TED: There's an apple tree in the garden.

SKULLY: There's an apple tree in every human garden. The problem is how to pluck the apple without breaking the twig. I'm an old man and I'm still learning.

TED: There's a girl coming up the path.

SKULLY: That's Eve. Looking for a friendly serpent. If you want to save your bacon, put on your running-shoes and get out of here. Her other name's Eila.

Knock on the door. SKULLY rises.

SKULLY: Come on in. *(EILA comes in.)*

EILA: I'm sorry. I didn't know there was someone with you.

SKULLY: That's all right, kid. *(to EILA)* Ted. *(to TED)* Eila.

TED: I'd better be making a move. The old man wants me to cut the hedge for him.

SKULLY: Don't go yet. We're not finished talking. Stay and have another cup of tea.

TED: I'd really better go. *(Moves towards door.)*

SKULLY: Well, if you must you must. But you can do a job for me. *(To EILA.)* Sit down kid. The boy won't bite. *(EILA sits down and smiles timidly at TED. SKULLY extracts a pound from his wallet.)* Here, you can put this on at the T.A.B. One quid double. Off the course. Trentham. Stormy Petrel and Rose of Kildare.

TED: I'll put it on now. Before they shut the window. I'll be seeing you, Skully. *(Smiles nervously at EILA and goes out.)*

SKULLY: Don't you think he's handsome? I bet you'd like to sit beside him in the pictures.

EILA: Yes.

SKULLY: What's he got that I haven't got?

EILA: He's young.

SKULLY: *(Nettled)* That's plain talking.

EILA: You've still got that dirty old skull! Why don't you chuck it

72

out in the rubbish tin? I don't like to see the head of a dead man looking at me. Bones and books together. There's no sense in it. Horrid old bones!

SKULLY: *(Still nettled)* It reminds me that I'm old. Too old to be friends with a girl of seventeen.

EILA: I didn't mean to hurt your feelings. *(Softening)* You're the best friend I've got really. But I wish you wouldn't prowl round me like a dog on the loose. It makes me jittery. Have you got a cigarette?

SKULLY lights a cigarette, puffs at it himself, places it in her mouth.

EILA: What did you do that for?

SKULLY: You asked me for a smoke.

EILA: I'm not your girlfriend. You'd better get that straight.

SKULLY: O.K. O.K. Keep your shirt on.

EILA: Dad says I mustn't come to see you any more. He says you're a menace.

SKULLY: What do you think?

EILA: I think you're nice. Except when you don't behave. I had a dream about you last night, Skully.

SKULLY: What was the dream? *(He sits down again.)*

EILA: I was in a big house. With hundreds of rooms. I don't know how I ever got there. Well, I heard people singing, and I went along a passage and down some stairs, and there was a party, with lots of beer and boys with guitars and a great big fire blazing in the centre of the room. I was awfully afraid it would burn the house down. But it wasn't doing any harm at all.

SKULLY: I'd like to have seen that fire.

EILA: Boys and girls were jiving all over the place. Jill was there. She had matador pants on and a green sweater, and her feet were bare, and her hair was hanging down. Colin was jiving with her. Every now and then, they'd dance right through the fire, and laugh like anything. It didn't hurt them one bit.

SKULLY: Where do I come into the dream?

EILA: I'm coming to that. I wanted so much for Colin to dance with me. I touched him on the shoulder, but he wouldn't take any notice. He just walked into the fire with Jill, and they didn't come out again. Then I began to cry in the dream. I ran out of the room and up a long flight of stairs. It was dreadfully lonely and dark. There was moonlight on the stair, shining through panes of glass, more like a church than a house. And great big empty corridors and cupboards full of clothes. I knew

Mum was waiting for me. I knew she'd be mad because I'd gone to the dance. In the dream I thought she was going to kill me. Then I saw you suddenly, standing at the top of the stair. Oh Skully, your face was lovely and kind and gentle! 'Don't worry,' you said, 'don't worry. No one's going to hurt you.' And then I woke up.

SKULLY: It wasn't such a bad dream after all.

EILA: If you'd always be the way you were in the dream, I wouldn't mind at all. I'd come up here and cook you scrambled eggs, and roll cigarettes for you, and we'd always be friends. Good friends.

SKULLY: There's two men inside me, Eila. One's a good old codger. Waiting for a harp and crown. He'd never harm a hair of your head. The other one's sad and bad and mad. He wants to grab hold of life with both hands. He's got hold of a tiger by the tail. How do you think I got this broken nose? I didn't get it playing marbles. The trouble is, I want you to like them both.

EILA: Well, I can't. It's no use asking. How did you get that way?

SKULLY: My mother never kissed me. Not once. She was a good Presbyterian. A very religious woman.

EILA: There's blood on your wrist. You must have cut it on a tin.

SKULLY: No. A woman bit me.

EILA: I don't blame her. I suppose you tried to make her go to bed with you.

SKULLY: Not exactly. She said it was a mark so I wouldn't forget her.

EILA: And will you forget her?

SKULLY: Not before Sunday. I've got a very short memory.

EILA: I wish you'd get rid of that skull. It annoys me every time I look at it.

SKULLY: *(Picks up skull, stands, walks about.)* It's the only certain friend I've got. A friend that never tells me off. Before Captain Cook sailed over the dry land at Miramar, this old skull was walking and talking and spearing fat pigeons. It looked at the sun and called itself a man. It could smell a woman's breath and the fug of a whare and the earth and the crushed fern leaves. It could hear the splash of a fish and the waves breaking on the shingle. It cursed and prayed and laughed and sang. It was a temple of the living God. And now there's no breath in its mouth. No tears in its eyes, only darkness. It stands for the last mystery. It saves me from believing that love or hate or fear or joy can last. It sets me free from the great human jail of hope. *(He rubs noses with the skull.)*

EILA: Oh! Put the filthy thing down!

SKULLY: One man's meat is another's poison. You'll look like that some day.

EILA: I hate it. I hate anything dead.

SKULLY: Death is the salt of life. Without death there'd be no resurrection.

EILA: You talk like a mad parson. I don't want to die; I want to go on living for ever and ever.

SKULLY: What's the great attraction? Is it Colin you want to live for? A boy in a leather jacket. With snot on his tie. Playing the guitar. Riding on a motorbike.

EILA: Yes. Colin. Or it might be someone else. And Colin doesn't wear a tie.

SKULLY: How did you run into him?

EILA: It was down at Halfmoon Bay. Jill and I went down there in the holidays. We were camping in a gully close to the beach. Every day I'd wake and hear the bellbirds ringing in the manuka. Like little silver bells. Then we'd go swimming or sailing or catching crayfish. I don't like crayfish.

SKULLY: They look like business men. Little black eyes and grinding pincers. Snap! Out and in from the hole in the rock. With a pound note in each claw. You can only see their feelers.

EILA: I didn't like the wetas either. Jill found a monster in her sleeping bag. She screamed until you could have heard her in Dunedin.

SKULLY: Maybe it wanted a bit of loving.

EILA: It should have found a lady weta then. Well, we soon found some boys were camped at the mouth of the creek. Half a mile away from us. We had a marvellous time. Riding the logs up and down in a little lagoon. Cooking sausages on sticks at a fire on the sand. Colin was the nicest of them all. He taught me to swim breaststroke.

SKULLY: I know that kind of teaching. You put your arm round like this — (He puts his arm round EILA, and hand on her breast. She stays still as if mesmerised. He kisses her. After ten seconds she breaks away violently.)

EILA: I hate you! I hate you! You spoil everything. You're nothing but a dirty old man.

SKULLY: Call me dirty if you like. But don't call me old.

EILA: You are old. You're old and horrible and ugly. Ugly! Ugly! Ugly!

She runs out, slamming door. SKULLY stands still.

CURTAIN

75

Saturday afternoon. SKULLY's room. SKULLY alone at the window.

SKULLY: It's a bright day. Sails on the harbour and the wind shaking the pine trees on the hill. That's where the couples go on a Saturday. There's many a girl up there with her pants full of needles ... Ma Bailey's hung her washing out. Poor old biddy. She deserves a gold medal ... You're a bloody fool, Skully, cooped up here like a dog. Waiting for a woman and a drunk. Why wait for anyone? *(He walks to the table and picks up the skull.)* You've stopped waiting. What's the answer, eh? You don't know. Or if you do, you can't tell. Dead bone. Dead, hollow bone. What's Hogan to me and you? And Norah? *(He walks back to the window.)* Hogan's my shadow. Hogan stops me forgetting the man I am. One drink and I'll be Hogan. And Norah's the tree with the golden apples on it. One touch and it withers to a stump.

He moves to the centre of the stage, with fists clenched at his sides.

Why did you make us? Why did you make us? Make us with a mind as big as the sky and a dirty hole to live in? When you made the sun and the moon, Jack Skully wasn't there. When you made the flying fish and the bloody great whale, Jack Skully wasn't even thought of. Except by you. You made him in your own time, and let him run wild and turn himself into a perambulating beer pump. And then you lifted him up and planted a new heart in his breast. I've cheated you a hundred times. Lying and bragging and humping. Forgetting all about you. *(He kneels.)* Give me a break, Father. Give me a break. I'm a bloody fool all right. You're the boss. Tell me what to do.

Knock at the door. SKULLY gets to his feet. FATHER TOM enters.

SKULLY: You're back, eh? What's the caper, Tom? What's on your mind?

FR. TOM: I met Hogan in town. He's got me worried. Drunk as a fiddler. Eyes like marbles and talking a lot of nonsense. About you, Skully. He sounded dangerous. You'd better not let him in the door. He should be in a strait-jacket.

SKULLY: Ah, Ben's only human. I'm not afraid of Ben.

FR. TOM: No one can help him now. I've watched him twenty years, going from bad to worse. Poor Ben. He was an altar boy,

76

and he trained to be a priest. He wasn't the man for it. No harm in that. But it left a kink in his mind somewhere. And then he took to the bottle.

SKULLY: Tom, I'm too old to try and separate the sheep from the goats. He comes to me for a quid and a place to lie down. I'll not refuse him that. A drunk's like a child. You can lead him but never push him. The trouble is you and your kind try to push Hogan into a box of your own making. If he'd never wanted to be a priest, maybe he wouldn't be a drunk now.

FR. TOM: He's a pushing man himself when he feels like it. The day he burgled the presbytery he nearly finished off the housekeeper. She can still show the finger-marks on her throat. But she's a good Christian soul and she wouldn't lay a charge against him.

SKULLY: That was a year ago. He's done his time.

FR. TOM: I'm not blaming Hogan. I'm just warning you that he's out of his mind.

SKULLY: You don't understand. Hogan and me belong to each other. I've been through the same routine myself. A barber's breakfast, the dry retches, a bottle of beer, and a cigarette. Sleeping in the shouse. Waking up too stiff to move. Day after day. Morning after morning. You think you know the ropes, Tom. You think you know everything, just because you're a priest. But you don't know the mind of a drunk.

FR. TOM: He's mad.

SKULLY: Where can you show me a man that's absolutely sane? Not you or me or Hogan. Don't worry, Tom. I'll stick by Hogan. He needs one friend that won't shut the door on him.

FR. TOM: Well, maybe you're right. But keep an eye on him. He knows how to use a club or a bottle. Goodbye. And God bless you.

SKULLY: I can handle Ben Hogan.

FATHER TOM nods and goes out slowly. SKULLY sits down at the table with his head in his hands. A pause. EILA enters silently. She now wears a ribbon and a ponytail hairstyle. She goes round behind SKULLY, without him seeing her, and places her hands over his eyes.

EILA: Guess. Who is it?

SKULLY: Norah . . . no . . . Eila!

EILA: Don't turn round. Now listen. I'm sorry I was cross. I didn't really mean what I said. But you made me cross by being silly. Are we friends now?

SKULLY: Of course. It was my fault. I should have known better.

EILA: All right then. *(She kisses the top of his head.)* That's to show there's no bad feelings left. You can turn around now.

SKULLY: *(Turning)* You've got a new ribbon in your hair. And who's the ponytail in honour of?

EILA: Never you mind. *(SKULLY puts his hands on her waist.)* Don't start that again!

SKULLY: *(Taking hands away)* O.K. So I'm still a menace.

EILA: I didn't say that. Just behave. Don't start pawing me again.

TED: *(From the outside)* Skully! Skully! *(He bursts in the door. SKULLY and EILA draw apart. TED throws his arm around SKULLY's shoulder.)* Skully, you beaut! You've struck it. You've struck the double.

SKULLY: The double? Oh, yes. How much was it, Ted?

TED: Three hundred smackers. Weren't you listening to the results?

SKULLY: I get sick of the radio. *(Light dawns on him.)* My God, that's better than chickenfeed! Three hundred on the nail. A case of Scotch and a foam-rubber mattress. No, no Scotch. But I'll be needing the mattress. Well, Ma Bailey'll be glad to hear it. So will Norah and Hogan. I'll tell the old girl first. *(He goes to the door and turns again.)* Stay here, you two. I'll be back in five minutes. *(He goes out.)*

TED and EILA take each other in.

TED: Here, take a chair.

EILA: Thank you. *(She sits.)*

TED: I'm glad the old boy won the double. He needs the money all right. What he doesn't spend on himself he gives away. I've seen him live on cold potatoes for a week.

EILA: Why didn't you help him out?

TED: I couldn't. I only get six quid a week myself. Wrapping newspapers. Mum takes half for board and banks thirty bob. That leaves me a lousy quid to play around with. Maybe you can't see the ball and chain *(he pats his ankle)* but I'm wearing one all right. You can't take a girlfriend out on a quid a week.

EILA: Some girls might pay their own share. If you explained it to them. Nicely.

TED: Not the ones I've met. Skully can do it, mind you. But he's fifty. He's got the technique.

EILA: Men make me tired! All you think about is technique. Technique. As if a girl was a new car. 'Shove in the clutch. No grinding in the gearbox. Smooth technique.' A girl wants to be treated like a human being . . .

TED: If a man treats a woman like a human being, she blames him for being slow. And if he plays the other game, she blames him for being fresh. You can't win out!

EILA: A woman's not a machine. That's why Skully can always get a girlfriend. He knows the difference.

TED: Why do *you* stick around with him. He's old enough to be your grandfather. I know you wouldn't find a better joker. As a friend, I mean. Someone to talk to when things get tough. But he's getting near the end of the road. Like one of those old sheets flapping in the wind.

EILA: Don't you dare talk about Skully like that! You ought to be ashamed of yourself. He's got more life in him than you'll ever have.

TED: How do you know that? *(He moves close to EILA.)* Come out with me tonight. There's a picture on at the Paramount. About the white slave traffic.

EILA: What makes you think I'd like that sort of picture?

TED: If you don't, we can try another one. Or go to a dance. Or just go down on the wharves and look at the moon.

EILA: No thanks. I've seen the moon a number of times. It always looks the same to me.

TED: You make it pretty tough. Have you got a boyfriend already?

EILA: No. Not exactly. I'm not going steady with anyone.

TED: I could borrow the old man's car. If he's not using it. We could go out to Moa Point or somewhere.

EILA: Why?

TED: You know why.

EILA: No, I don't! And if I do, it's none of your business. You're in too much of a hurry, Mr Clever. We only met this morning.

TED: *(Moving away again)* All right. All right. There's no harm in asking.

EILA: It depends on the way you ask.

TED: Women are all the same. You want a red carpet laid down. And a band playing 'Annie Laurie'. And everything that opens and shuts. It takes money, money. That's all a man needs. Plenty of money.

EILA: If that's what you think, you're welcome to think it. *(More gently.)* How long ago did you learn to drive?

TED: A year and a half ago. My cobber Max had an old truck, and he taught me in it. Max lives up in the King Country. He's got a farm there. South of Taumarunui. I remember we had a smashup . . . but you wouldn't be interested.

EILA: Go on. Please.

TED: Well, we had a big load of wood on the back. Ten o'clock at night. Max and me in the cab together. And we came down the track at forty. The brakes weren't too good. Max slams them on just as we come round the bend and the bridge was in sight. The bridge over the creek below his farm. Max was half full of booze. She skidded this way and that, and turned a half circle, and shot right into the creek above the bridge . . .

EILA: *(Laughs)* I wish I'd been there. What did you do?

TED: We climbed out and sat on the roof of the cab and waited till morning. The top of the cab was just out of water. Max had a bottle of rum in his pocket, and we cleaned that up before the daylight came. Singing every song that we could remember. The headlights were still on under water, and you could see the eels swimming round them.

EILA: I'll go out with you tonight. But you'll have to drive a lot better than that.

TED: What made you change your mind? *(He comes close and puts his hand on her shoulder. She places her own hand gently on it. SKULLY enters. TED draws back.)*

SKULLY: You're a fast worker, Mr Hardwick. No, don't worry about me. There's a bedroom through the door. Do you want the loan of a frogskin?

EILA: You're not being fair. Ted and I . . .

SKULLY: It's 'Ted and I', is it? All right. The young go off with the young. That's the way it should be. But not on my doorstep. Go on. Shift. *(EILA shifts.)* Get the hell out of here. *(TED follows.)*

TED: Eila . . . Eila!

A pause. SKULLY sits down. MA BAILEY appears in the doorway.)

MA BAILEY: I'm glad those two have gone. Like two tadpoles in a jar together. All head and gills. The young people now have got no sense of what's right. Roaring round on motor bikes at two in the morning. Girls dressed like boys, and boys like nothing at all. I like a man to look a man.

SKULLY: Fashions change, Ma. Not people. People don't change. Remember the old dance hall. With kerosene lamps hanging on the rafters. Or was that before your time? And the keg around the back, and the track worn down to the lupins. We had the same idea. The same as the kids do now. A kiss and a cuddle and the old game of hunt-the-thimble.

MA BAILEY: Did they try to get money out of you? All they care about is money.

SKULLY: Who cares about money? Money's a slow poison. I've seen more men killed by money than with guns or booze or women.

MA BAILEY: You've got to find a use for it. I'm going to get myself a new hat and a pair of blue bedroom slippers. With the twelve pound ten I won on Stormy Petrel. You told me to back it, Mr Skully. What are you going to get yourself? Three hundred's a lot of money.

SKULLY: A foam-rubber mattress.

MA BAILEY: And what else?

SKULLY: I've not got a clue. Booze is out. Maybe I'll take a trip.

MA BAILEY: You should ask the spirits.

SKULLY: Spirits? What spirits? The only spirits I know is gin, whisky, brandy, meths. Or maybe spirits of salt.

MA BAILEY: Hush! Don't joke about it. The spirits don't like people joking about them.

SKULLY: Who taught you this game of spirits?

MA BAILEY: Connie did.

SKULLY: Connie? *(Laughs)* That skinny old bag on stilts! She should have a broomstick to ride on. She's a witch all right. Haven't you seen her, on a stormy day, crossing the harbour, riding in a sieve? She killed her husband as well. Tied his doodle in a knot. He died of a full bladder and a broken heart.

MA BAILEY: Don't laugh, Mr Skully. Connie and I play the game with a glass. The spirits tell us what to do. One rap for yes, two raps for no. Every night we play it at the kitchen table.

SKULLY: *(Takes a glass from the shelf)* Well, here's your glass. Nine-pence at Woolworths. What do you do now?

MA BAILEY: Sit down. Opposite me. *(They sit at the table with the upturned glass between them.)* Let your fingers rest on the glass. No, rest them gently. *(Both rest the tips of their fingers on the glass.)* Now, hold my hand. *(They grip with free hands: right and left respectively.)* Now, think of nothing. Give it time for the power to come into the glass. *(Pause.)* Look! It's moving already. It wants to talk. I've never known it to start so quickly. Ask it a question, Mr Skully.

SKULLY: Who are you?

MA BAILEY: No, you can't ask that. Ask it a question where it can say yes or no.

SKULLY: Is it good for me to strike the double? *(Glass gives one sharp rap.)*

MA BAILEY: Yes. It says yes. Go on asking.

SKULLY: Will I keep the money long? *(Two raps.)* No? Tell me, is Hogan mad? *(Two raps.)* No? That's one in the eye for Father

Tom. Should I let Hogan come here? *(One rap.)* Yes. Will somebody stick to me? You know the one I mean. *(Two raps.)* No? That's bad news. You're moving the glass, Ma!

MA BAILEY: I'm not. It's jumping under my fingers.

SKULLY: O.K. I'll believe it. Am I going to live to be sixty? *(One rap.)* That's good. To be seventy? *(One rap.)* Better still. Eighty? *(Two raps.)* No. Well, they reckon the last ten years are the worst. Where do you come from? Are you someone dead? *(No movement of glass.)* It's not moving.

MA BAILEY: I told you you can't ask who it is. That annoys it and sends it away.

SKULLY: Well, that's enough for today. Hogan's not mad. The money's going to burn a hole in my pocket. I'll live to a ripe old age.

MA BAILEY: There was another answer too.

SKULLY: We'll forget that one. I shouldn't have asked it. Well, you've proved your point, Ma. Glasses can talk. I thought they could only ring. When you strike them with a finger-nail. What's that? It'll be Norah and Hogan, I'll bet.

Noise of stumbling offstage. NORAH and HOGAN enter. HOGAN is very drunk.

SKULLY: *(Rising)* Well, here's company. *(He seizes NORAH, lifts her under knees and waist, and carries her.)* I've caught an opossum! Who'll buy its skin. Ah, you beauty!

NORAH: Put me down, you bloody fool. *(She is not displeased. HOGAN is.)*

SKULLY: By God, you're a weight, Norah. *(He sets her down.)* I think you must be in pod.

MA BAILEY: I can see I'm not wanted here. *(She rises, goes to door, and turns.)* You mind, Mr Skully. They won't do you any good. They're only after your money. *(Savagely)* Go on! Turn the place into a pigsty. But if you start shouting I'll call the police. *(She goes out.)*

HOGAN: *(Singing)*

> Veni, Sancte Spiritus,
> Et emitte caelitus
> Lucis tuae radium . . .

That old pelican's got you taped, Skully. You ought to have clouted her one. *(Threatens SKULLY.)* Keep your bloody hands off Norah! She's cost me ten beers and three gins today already.

NORAH: You're a liar, Ben. I paid for my own drinks. And half of
yours, as well.

SKULLY: You're just a bludger. Take a look at yourself. When did
you last have a shave?

HOGAN: They don't have a barber's shop in the Basin Reserve.
(Pause.) Who put the johns onto me? Eh, Skully? You've got it
all worked out. Tell me that one.

SKULLY: How should I know? The priest must have rung them up.
It's your own bloody fault. What do you have to go burgling in
daylight for?

NORAH: Ah, you're like a couple of dogs! Give it a rest. *(To
SKULLY.)* You know bloody well why Ben bust the window in
daylight. To get money. He'd got no money. If you don't get
money, you don't eat. If you don't eat, you die. I'd bust more
than a window to dodge that old man there. *(She points to the
skull.)*

SKULLY: *(Slowly)* I struck the double today. Three hundred quid.

HOGAN: You struck the double! You old devil!

SKULLY: Stormy Petrel and Rose of Kildare.

HOGAN: I put ten bob on Armageddon. For a place. The bastard
ran backwards.

NORAH: *(Putting her arms round SKULLY)* Skully, I am glad. Let's
get a bottle and celebrate.

HOGAN: The woman goes to the man with the money.

SKULLY: Stop croaking, you bloody frog! You'll get your share of
the whisky.

HOGAN: And the woman too.

NORAH: Shut your mouth, Hogan!

HOGAN: I'll cut your gizzard out. *(He springs at NORAH. SKULLY
catches him from behind with an arm round his throat. A
struggle. HOGAN falls.)*

SKULLY: *(Benging over HOGAN)* He's out to it. By God, he's got a
powerful grip on him. It's a wonder. His arms are as thin as a
flax-stick.

NORAH: Get a cushion, Skully. *(SKULLY gets the cushion.)* Here,
put it under his head. *(They arrange the cushion under,
HOGAN'S head.)* Poor Ben. He's gone out like a light. He can't
hold his grog any more. He wanted to lie down and sleep on the
floor of the Brunswick.

SKULLY: Maybe you should have left him to it.

NORAH: I couldn't do that. The johns would have picked him up.

SKULLY: Let him sleep. He'll wake up right as rain.

NORAH: He's getting worse than he used to be. He'll do you harm
one day, Skully.

SKULLY: Not Hogan. I know his mind better than I do my own. Ben's a child. A big, ugly child. With all the rages and the lonely heart of a child. Look at him sleeping, quiet as an angel. I've taken him into my own bed, Norah, when you could shovel the frost up with a spade. He had the shakes and couldn't hold a teacup. And I nursed him back for another round on the grog. He doesn't bear any malice either. He won't remember anything when he wakes.

NORAH: Have it your own way then. Hogan's a bad bargain. But what were you and the old lady up to? A minute ago when I opened the door? You jumped up as if you'd been shot. You were holding hands, weren't you?

SKULLY: We were playing a game with a glass.

NORAH: With a glass? What game's that?

SKULLY: Spirits. She reckons the spirits make the glass move.

NORAH: And did they?

SKULLY: If they didn't, I've got the shakes myself. Or else she has.

NORAH: You shouldn't do it. It's not safe.

SKULLY: What do you mean — 'safe'?

NORAH: The Church doesn't allow it.

SKULLY: What the hell does the Church know about it? You're back in the Middle Ages. I thought you'd broken with them. A lot of bloody nonsense.

NORAH: Maybe. Maybe not.

SKULLY: Once a Doolan always a Doolan. You've got holy water on the brain.

NORAH: It's still not safe. If there's a katipo under a stone, it's better not to lift it.

SKULLY: Katipos and holy water! *(He puts his hand to his forehead.)* My head's aching. *(He sits down.)* Put your hands on my forehead, Norah. There's an iron band around it, and someone's screwing it tighter. *(Norah stands beside him, with hands round his forehead.)* Ah, that's better. It's easing off. You've got the healing touch all right. Your father must have been a *tohunga.*

NORAH: He wasn't. He was a bloody Irish pig.

SKULLY: Norah——*(He swivels the chair.)* Come closer. *(He grips her between his knees, hands on waist.)* You're a sight for sore eyes. I've got you in my blood, Norah. You're the sunlight in the morning. You're the high tide and the seventh wave. The one that breaks above the sandhills and floods the old dry grass-roots. Norah, let's get out of here, you and me. You're a woman in a thousand. *(She smiles at him.)* Marry me, Norah.

You'll never regret the day. *(She bends forward and kisses him. He pulls her down on his knee.)*

I may be old, but there's plenty of life in me yet. We'll go up North and start a boarding house. No bludgers allowed. A tea and tray in the morning. You'd look well in an apron. And you can have kids. As many kids as you like. Eight of them——*(She jerks away from him and stands rigid.)* What the hell's gone wrong with you?

NORAH: *(Slowly)* No kids. I don't want kids. Not ever. I don't want to have a kid.

SKULLY: What's the matter? You've gone grey in the face.

NORAH: Oh, don't ask me! Leave me alone! Leave me alone! *(She sits in the other chair, puts her head on the table and weeps.)*

SKULLY: *(Rising and putting his hand on her shoulder)* O.K. O.K. Take it easy now. No kids then. Just the two of us.

NORAH: *(Recovering slightly)* I'm sorry, Skully. Oh, I'm sorry. We'd never make a go of it.

SKULLY: You reckon I'm too old?

NORAH: Not too old. You've got what it takes. But I don't want to marry you.

SKULLY: Why not? If you want a Church marriage, you can have it. With bells and a priest. I don't care if you get the Pope's blessing. You'll still be the same under the sheet.

NORAH: *(Sitting up)* It's not that. But we **will** change. You'll be an old man down at the bowling green. With one foot in the grave. Smoking a pipe and talking about nothing. And I'll be at home, cleaning the kitchen stove. Waiting to nag you when you come in. Each of us waiting to die. Each in our own little box. Hating each other and blaming each other because nothing ever happens any more. Except the priest coming round to say Hullo. Or Mrs Murphy breaking her ankle. Or who won the Test, who killed who, how much is butter, how much is tea! I've watched it happen and I know what it's like. Marriage is worse than murder. Murder is quick. We're better off the way we are.

SKULLY: Maybe you're right. I went up to Mount Cook once and stayed at the pub there. Mountains all around. And a mountain of bottles in the gully at the back. Well, one day I thought I'd take a stroll. And I came to a place where a signpost stood. One sign read—'To the Stocking Glacier'—another—'To Mount Sefton'—another—'To the Ball Hut'—and so on—but I thought I'd be smart. I took the road that hadn't got a sign up. It landed me in the place where they kept the pigs. That's life in a nutshell.

85

NORAH: I'll stick by you.

SKULLY: What about the sailors?

NORAH: I don't need the sailors if I can stay with you. *(She gets up and goes to SKULLY.)* Oh, Skully! I like you better than anyone. Let's laugh a bit. You look as if you'd fallen from a hearse. Look, I'll teach you to waltz. *(They move around the stage, NORAH lightly, SKULLY awkwardly.)*
No, you'll never make a good dancer. Well, there's more to life than dancing. *(She embraces him.)*

SKULLY: Careful now. I'm not made of asbestos. There's a dog here ready to bark at you.

NORAH: I like dogs. *(Embrace.)* Come on in. He won't wake for an hour yet.

SKULLY and NORAH go into the bedroom. They embrace standing. NORAH begins to unbutton SKULLY's shirt.

CURTAIN

ACT III

Monday evening. SKULLY, NORAH and HOGAN are sitting in SKULLY's shack with a bottle of whisky.

HOGAN: Why the hell don't you drink, Skully? You paid for it. A couple of glasses would put a shine on your knob.

NORAH: Don't be a fool, Ben. One drink might put him in his grave.

HOGAN: I'm not afraid of it. Up on the Island I had to squeeze out the juice from a tin of boot polish. There's a great wide country inside a bottle. With stars above and rivers down below . . .

He rises and sings, with appropriate actions:

> I was full as a bull on Flanagan's rum,
> Not even a ribbon to cover me bum,
> When I climbed on a branch of the old apple tree
> And opened the window of Sally Magee.

> Oh, Sally Magee she was brown as a nut,
> She could spit like a tiger and bark like a pup —
> But the thing she liked best was a hand on her knee —
> *lays his hand on NORAH's knee*
> For a loveable woman was Sally Magee.

86

Her bandy old husband forbade me the house —
Poor angel, he led her the life of a louse —
And I swore by the sky that avenged I'd be
And ride with no bridle sweet Sally Magee.

With diamonds and rubies I did not adore her
But the serpent of Moses I brandished before her —
brandishes fist appropriately

SKULLY: Cut it out, Ben. You're shouting like an auctioneer.

NORAH: *(To SKULLY)* Hit him on the head with a brick!

HOGAN: *(Sitting down)* You're a sour little bitch. First you play a man along like a fish. Then you tell someone to hit him on the head. It's the Maori blood in you.

NORAH: Dirty bloody pakehas! What do you know about being a Maori?

SKULLY: I wasn't so dirty on Saturday when you wanted a quid off me. You called me husband then.

NORAH: Keep your bloody quids. What's a quid between you and me?

HOGAN: A quid's twenty beers.

SKULLY: There's no **apartheid** in this house. I don't give a bugger if your mother was an Eskimo. You started it, Hogan.

HOGAN: Ah, she's touchy!

NORAH: You'd be touchy if you'd had the dirt rubbed in from the time you were so high. By every tin can boss and drunken ape.

SKULLY: The tuis tried the hawk to kill —
Kapai Te Rauparaha!
And yet the hawk is living still —
Kapai Te Rauparaha!
The hawk can soar, the hawk can fight,
Kapai Te Rauparaha!
The hawk will have a feast tonight,
Kapai Te Rauparaha!

NORAH: Te Rauparaha—he's a long time dead. You know what they say in books. Speeches on the **marae**. Granny Te Puea. The fine Maori race. All sitting under the pohutukawa tree. Waiting for the tree to fall. Maori and Pakeha. All in the same canoe. *(Savagely.)* Balls! What do I get out of it? A kick in the guts.

SKULLY: Have a drink and forget it.

NORAH: You reckon, eh? I go up the Terrace and look for a room. Rain pissing down. The old fat sow she opens the door. Face to make the devil run. 'You want a room, eh?' 'I want a room.'

'How much can you pay?' 'Two quid maybe.' 'Rooms are three pounds ten with a gas ring.' 'O.K. I'll take it.' 'Are you a clean person?' 'What do you mean? I wash every day.' 'The last Maori girl I had, she wasn't clean. She had men in as well.' 'You can stuff your room. I'd rather sleep in the park.' She slams door right in my face.

SKULLY: No more sleeping in the park. Not with three hundred in the kitty. What about a trip to Taupo, Norah?

NORAH shakes her head.

SKULLY: Why not, eh?

NORAH: My father came from Taupo.

SKULLY: Well, who cares? We've got the dough anyway. The priest gave me the tip. Trust a priest to know where the kale grows. Drink up, Hogan! I'll get another bottle when this one's dry.

HOGAN: *(Standing)* I'll have a hose instead. Where's the House of Commons?

SKULLY: Out the door and round the back. Take care of the seat. It's broken at the hinges. *(HOGAN shambles out.)* Hogan's got his eye on you. I wouldn't trust him with a tomcat.

NORAH: Ben's all right. It's just the booze talking.

SKULLY: He's never been off it in the time I've known him. Except in clink or on the Island.

NORAH: He reckons you put the johns on his track. After he burgled the presbytery.

SKULLY: The bloody maniac. I'm the best friend he's got. I'd never put the johns onto any man. Least of all Hogan. He's all in the dark like Poor Blind Nell. *(Loud crash at the back.)* What the hell's he up to? He must have slipped off the seat.

NORAH: Go and see if he's hurt.

SKULLY: No bloody fear. He'd crack me as soon as look. He'll be fighting mad.

The door is flung open. HOGAN enters wearing the lavatory seat round his neck like a collar.

HOGAN: With diamonds and rubies I did not adore her
But the serpent of Moses I brandished before her —
(brandishes fist)
'Oh, Paddy,' she murmured, 'a gentleman be!'
But she winked as she said it, did Sally Magee.

SKULLY: Take the collar off, Hogan. You're not cut out for Holy Orders.

88

HOGAN: Oh, Time is a feather that's quick in its falling!
I left her alone when the red east was dawning —
While the waves of the Shannon run down to the sea
I'll always remember sweet Sally Magee.

NORAH: Give it a rest, Ben. You're bellowing the roof off. There's a whisky left in the bottle.

SKULLY: Be quiet, man. You're not on the stage.

HOGAN: *(Pulls seat over head, goes towards SKULLY, brandishing seat as weapon)* I'll kill you, Skully! You put the demons onto me. I'll kill you for that.

HOGAN grapples with SKULLY. SKULLY seizes seat and sends it spinning across the stage.

SKULLY: Ah, shut up, Ben! There's no sense left in your head.

MA BAILEY bursts door open and steps inside.

MA BAILEY: I'll not stand it! I'll not stand it!

HOGAN: Oh, it's me grandmother's ghost! *(He drops down in chair, head on arms.)*

MA BAILEY: Mr Skully. You've got to go. I've had as much as any woman can stand. Trouble, trouble, trouble! Last year they cut my kidney out. The doctor said it wasn't a stone I'd got inside me, it was a quarry. What good is a quarry to me? I thought when I took you in—'Here's a gentleman,' I thought, 'he may look rough, but he'll pay attention to a woman's feelings. Now I can have a bit of peace.' And what's the answer? Noise, noise, noise! Day after day and night after night. Drunken blackguards and filthy women!

NORAH: Filthy women! You're jealous. You wanted to have Skully to yourself. Sewing on a coat button. Rubbing up against him. He's mine, I tell you, mine!

SKULLY: I don't belong to you or her. Jack Skully is his own master.

MA BAILEY: There's no peace, no peace! All I want is a bit of peace. They're letting off hydrogen bombs in Australia. Poisoning the world. What's going to happen to the little people — the people that want a bit of peace? A house and a warm bed, and a man home at 5 o'clock, putting his arm around you and telling you there's no time like the present. And a Christmas tree at Christmas. And scones in the oven. Hot white scones with currants and butter. And someone to tell you he likes them. But the world's changed all around. It's black and old and poisoned.

Poison inside of us, making us sad and bad and wicked. Poor Andy's in his grave—and I'm an old, sick woman waiting for the undertaker. With you, and you, and you, shouting and drinking and fighting and poisoning the lovely night. Pigs in a dirty sty. What's that. What's that on the floor? *(She crosses stage and picks up lavatory seat.)*

SKULLY: Hogan was wearing it. Give it a bone, Ma! Live and let live. I was trying to make him tone down.

MA BAILEY: Oh, it's the last straw! Out you go, Mr Skully! Out . . . you . . . go! *(She seizes him by the shoulders and tries to run him out the door.)*

NORAH: *(Seizing her)* You can't do that. He's paid the rent for a fortnight.

MA BAILEY: *(Letting go SKULLY, turning on NORAH)* All right. All right then. He's paid the rent. And what about you, my lady? I rented this place to Mr Skully. Not to a Maori prostitute.

NORAH slaps her face.

MA BAILEY: Oh! Oh! Oh! *(She goes to the door, then turns again.)* I'm going to get the police.

SKULLY: You shouldn't have done that, Norah. She'd have cooled off in a minute or two. Now, I'll have to go and soothe her down again.

NORAH: A lot you care about me! You heard what she said. I should have pulled her eyes out! You can go to hell, Skully. *(SKULLY approaches her.)* Don't you come near me!

SKULLY goes out. HOGAN rises swaying.

HOGAN: Norah, me jewel. Where's the ladder up to Heaven? The ladder with the golden rungs. The Devil stole it while we were hugging and kissing and fighting and snoring and drinking. Under the apple tree. He carried it off and buried it a thousand miles in the ground. No one can find it. Not me or you or the Pope of Rome. The saint on his knees and the poor black-handed sinner. I wish I was holy Brendan in his boat of stone. I'd sail and find it, Norah. You and me together. We'd lie down merry in the cradle of the sea. Oh, I'm burning, I'm burning! The fire of Gehenna is eating me alive. Give me the bottle, Norah.

NORAH: The bottle's empty. Go into the room and lie down there and sleep.

HOGAN: Lie down beside me. Norah. I've got the shakes.

NORAH: Not on your sweet life. I'm waiting here for Skully. You

90

go and sleep and wake up sober. *(She shoves him into the bedroom. He falls full length on the bed. She comes out, wanders round the room, picks up the skull and dances with it)*

NORAH: *(Singing)*

> O you're my darling, you're my bony darling,
>> O you are the strong one, the robber of my dreams,
> You're my one and only. Kiss me when I'm lonely,
>> The prettiest husband that ever was seen.

> Tell me then truly, my husband, my only,
>> Is it cold in the gully where bone touches bone?
> Is there room for another, my fancy, my father,
>> Or do they sleep old there and always alone?

She sits down at the table with the skull in her lap. TED comes in timidly.

NORAH: What do you want? Skully's not home.

TED: I . . . I was hoping for a bit of company.

NORAH: You've come to the wrong house then.

TED: I'm not sure. We met on Saturday, didn't we?

NORAH: If you call it meeting. You came in the door and I went out.

TED: I thought you were very beautiful.

NORAH: Look, mister. Don't get any big ideas. What's your name anyway?

TED: Ted Hardwick.

NORAH: What did you want to see Skully about?

TED: Just to say Hullo. I like Skully. We've been cobbers a long time.

NORAH: Cobbers! You and Skully could never be cobbers. Skully's a man.

TED: What do you think I am?

NORAH: I don't know and I don't care.

TED: *(Goes forward, takes chair, sits straddling it, close to NORAH)* Look, Norah —

NORAH: Miss Vane to you. Who told you my name was Norah?

TED: Skully did.

NORAH: What else did he tell you about me?

TED: Nothing much.

NORAH: Something. Something you've got in your mind.

TED: He told me you go down on the boats.

NORAH: O.K. You reckoned I'd go to bed with you instead of a sailor?

91

TED: I reckoned you might. Why not? My money's as good as theirs.

NORAH: Not on your sweet life.

TED: I don't get it. You go to bed with Hogan. With Skully. With a Liverpool Irishman from Abadan. But you won't go to bed with me.

NORAH: *(Smiling enticingly)* How much dough had you got for me, eh, boy?

TED: I'd have given you a fiver.

NORAH: Give it to me now.

TED: Here. It's all I've got.

NORAH: Come here, big boy. *(She puts skull back on table and stands up.)* Give me a kiss.

TED comes forward, puts his arms clumsily round her. She remains wooden while he kisses her. Then she gives him a shove that sends him sprawling to the floor. HOGAN rises in the bedroom.

NORAH: O.K. You've had all you're going to get. *(She tears the money into small pieces and throws it at him.)* This bitch is not on heat.

TED: What do you mean?

NORAH: You think you're bloody smart. You thought I'd be an easy make. A Maori bag. Hot stuff.

TED: I never said that.

NORAH: No. You only thought it. You thought you could buy me with five lousy quid. Just like buying a pork chop. You forgot that I was a human being. The dirty bloody sailors need me. Skully needs me. That old scabby drunk needs me. He's down in the mud and he can't get up. You don't need me. You only think you do.

HOGAN enters: steadier on his feet.

HOGAN: What's the score? Who's that? I'll plug him for you.

NORAH: Leave him alone, Ben. He's had his lesson already. School's over for the day.

TED: You've won this round all right. With a fancy man to back you up.

HOGAN: I'll crack him one.

NORAH: Let him go. *(To TED.)* Go back home and kiss your mother goodnight. I'm not a teddy bear. *(TED goes quickly out.)* Ah Ben, I'm tired! Tired of living.

HOGAN: Sit down, Norah. *(She moves to sit on chair.)* No, not there, down here. Get close to the ground and there's no fear of falling. *(She sits on the floor. He lies beside her, his head on her knee.)* Put your hand on me forehead. It's heavy as a stone.

NORAH: Take it easy, Ben. Come down from the Cross. Here now, put your head in my lap. If you'd leave the meths alone, you might do some good for yourself. Ah, look at the stars. They're shining through the branches of the tree.

HOGAN: There's a mountain on me heart. It's dark where I am, Norah. There's peace for the dead. There's peace for the whole black world, but no peace for Hogan. There's light at the window now. There's light in every house, but no light where Hogan is. Wash the blood from me hands and feet. Put your hand in me side, Norah. I've got an everlasting wound.

NORAH: *(Bending over his face and kissing his forehead)* Can you hear me, Ben? The johns have gone off duty. With their great black boots and their wooden faces and their rubber pipes—

HOGAN: They had me in a cell and they was beating Christ out of me. With the handcuffs on, so I couldn't move me arms. There was Lonie and Ryan and Tiger Smith. Taking turns. There was blood on the wall, but not much blood. The johns have got it down to a fine art. They can pound you crazy and never leave a mark. Then a demon sticks his head in the door. 'Give him one for me, boys,' he says. 'I been waiting a long time for this.' Then Ryan up and lets drive and punches me right in the guts. The demon pretty near died of laughing. Next day the Beak was tough. He reckoned I should be jailed for life. And he slammed on a month for resisting arrest.

NORAH: Never mind. It's over now. The bad job's done, and you and me alone, love, like the day that you were born. I'm your mother and you a boy again.

HOGAN: Ah, your voice is like a waterfall. It's melting the rock around me heart. Norah, let's go from here. Where did Skully put his money? We'll need a bit of money.

NORAH: Maybe I'll go with you. Maybe I'll stay with Skully. Just you be quiet. What's that on the path outside? It's the step of someone coming. It'll be Skully. Get up, Ben. You go and rest now—

A knock at the door.

Go on, Ben. Put your head down and you'll be right. *(She leads him like a child to the bedroom, holding hands, lifts first one leg, then the other onto the bed, comes out and closes bedroom door.)* Just a minute. I'm coming.

FATHER TOM enters. NORAH steps back in surprise.

NORAH: Good evening, Father. I'd forgotten you said you might call.

FR. TOM: I knew I'd find you, child. Sit down again. *(Both sit.)* How long is it since you made your last confession?

NORAH: Eight years, Father. But you're making a mistake. I'm not going to confess to you.

FR. TOM: No, no, of course not. Who is in the next room?

NORAH: Ben Hogan. He's sick with the drink.

FR. TOM: God is alive in Skully and crucified in Hogan. You love them dearly, don't you, child? *(NORAH nods.)* You must learn to love them in God's way, not your own.

NORAH: Don't preach at me. I've heard it all before.

FR. TOM: You've got a generous heart. Use it for God, and not against Him. The power of a woman's love is very great, for good or evil . . .

NORAH: What do you know of a woman's love?

FR. TOM: The woman under the Cross, with grey hair and a broken heart, holding the body of her mangled Son. Only the naked can clothe the naked. Only the wounded can heal another's wounds. There is a fountain of great love at the bottom of your heart. Don't let it run away in the dry sand. Don't let it come to nothing.

NORAH: You're a good man, but you don't know me, Father. I've lost the Faith.

FR. TOM: Now that was a great pity. How did you come to lose it?

NORAH: It's not your concern. I've finished with the Church.

FR. TOM: Ah, but has the Church finished with you? A mother is still a mother, even when the child has repudiated her.

NORAH: What kind of a mother was the Church to me? When I was fifteen they sent me to Reformatory.

FR. TOM: You must have made some bad mistake.

NORAH: I'd been sleeping with a married man. My mother was dead. My father used to thrash me with the buckle of his belt.

FR. TOM: So you needed more love than they gave you. Well, in the eyes of God maybe it wasn't a crime.

NORAH: I couldn't stand being shut in.

FR. TOM: It's hard for a young creature.

NORAH: Those bloody old women with their cardboard faces! What do they know about being alive? Three times I ran away, and they brought me back again. Then I smashed the bed in my room—and they locked me up where no one ever came.

FR. TOM: And so you doubted the mercy of God.

NORAH: Oh, what's the use, what's the use! It's all done now.

FR. TOM: What happened to the man?

NORAH: He went off to Australia. A man can run away, but a woman's got to stay and face the music.

FR. TOM: And what about the child?

NORAH: Who said there was a child?

FR. TOM: There was a child.

NORAH: *(Head down on the table)* You're driving me mad! Oh for Jesus' sake leave me alone! Take the Church with you. Take the saints and the angels and the wood of the Cross, God and His Blessed Mother, and bundle them up in a blanket and chuck them into the middle of the sea. Leave me alone. I only want to be left alone!

FR. TOM: Hell's being on your own. You told me that on Saturday. Is the child alive or dead?

NORAH: Dead, Father, dead. Dead, dead, dead. *(From now on she speaks very quietly)*.

FR. TOM: Be easy now. The child is with God. Was it ever baptised?

NORAH: I baptised it. Then I covered its face with a blanket and let it die. I killed my own child.

FR. TOM: *(Stands and lays a hand on her head)* Ah, now you can be at peace. Poor woman, that's a great cold sin to carry all alone.

NORAH: It was so small, so small. It only wanted milk and a cuddle and a place to lie down.

FR. TOM: It is over now. The child is in heaven. There is no more need for grief. Are you ready to make your confession? *(NORAH nods. He seats himself)*. Kneel down beside me then. *(She kneels beside his chair.)*

FR. TOM: *(Blesses her)* In the name of the Father and of the Son and of the Holy Ghost . . . What sins have you committed since your last confession? *(NORAH is silent.)* You've committed murder?

NORAH: Yes, Father.

FR. TOM: And you've doubted the Faith and let the Devil bring you to despair?

NORAH: Yes, Father.

FR. TOM: And you've been angry many times? and stayed away from Holy Mass?

NORAH: Yes, Father.

FR. TOM: And you've stolen money? and been lazy? and been drunken and gluttonous?

NORAH: Yes, Father.

FR. TOM: And you've committed many sins of impurity with yourself and with others? With men and women?

NORAH: Yes, Father.

FR. TOM: Is there any other sin that you're bound to confess?

NORAH: I told lies about another girl. I said she was a thief when it wasn't true at all. And I struck an old woman on the face.

FR. TOM: Any other sin, my child?

NORAH: I've taken the Holy Name in vain.

FR. TOM: Is there anything more you have to confess?

NORAH: No, Father.

FR. TOM: All right then. Thank God for letting you make such a good confession. You will have to give back the money you have stolen. And go to the people you lied to and tell them the truth. You must keep away from any man who might be an occasion of sin for you. You will know in your own heart when that is the case. If you must meet such a man, let it be in the company of others. Have you got a firm intention to do this?

NORAH: Yes, Father.

FR. TOM: I'm sure you have. Think of Our Lord in the arms of His Blessed Mother after He came down from the Cross. Remember that your sins are the cause of His agony and death. Tell Him that you're sorry for all your sins. And for your penance say one Our Father and one Hail Mary. Now make a good act of contrition.

NORAH: O my God, I am very sorry . . . *(very softly)*

FR. TOM: *(Simultaneously)* **Ego te absolvo** . . . *(To the audience his* **Ego te absolvo** *is heard clearly, the rest of the absolution and NORAH's act of contrition is not.)* Go in peace, my child. And pray for me, a sinner.

NORAH rises. FATHER TOM then kneels down before her.

NORAH: Father! Father! Stand up. You shouldn't be kneeling.

FR. TOM: *(Still on his knees)* Your soul is pure now, child. As pure as it was after baptism. There's no sin left in your heart, by the power of the sacrament of mercy. And I am full of sin. A priest without merit. *(He rises.)*
It's terrible thing to be a shepherd of souls, when your own soul is blind and deaf and dumb. *(Listens.)* Ah, it's raining, child. It's the good rain falling. Falling on pub and shop and house and church and monastery and graveyard. The ground is thirsty too. It opens its mouth and drinks like a thirsty man. And the water swells the wheat grain and raises it up . . . .

Listen, Elias,
To the winter rain . . .
For the seed sleeps
By the sleeping stone,
But the seed has life
While the stone has none . . .

Come with me. You mustn't sleep in this house.

NORAH: Yes, Father. *(They both go out.)*

Pause. HOGAN comes slowly onto a dark stage.

HOGAN: Norah! Norah! Norah, where are you? Ah, the bloody moll! She's gone off and left me to suffer. There should be a wee drop left in the bottle. *(He crosses stage, takes bottle, drinks from it.)* No more than would wet your tongue. If I had the dough, I'd be drinking in Blaney's now. *(Sits down, clasps hands round knees, leans forward.)*

Skull on table brightens. A green or blue light inside skull. The rest of the stage dark. A round light on HOGAN.

VOICE: Hogan! Hogan!

HOGAN: Who's that? Oh, it's you, me bony friend. Don't come near, or I'll smash you to smithereens. I thought you was one of the demons. Are you mad or is it me?

VOICE: I'm dead. And you'll be dead. For a long, long time, Hogan.

HOGAN: Well, that's news! There's no harm done. A man was born to die. It's the road between that's dark and heavy going. Give me an empty railway carriage, with Concrete Grady at me head and Old Snowy Lindsay at me feet. And a bottle of plonk to pass between us. Then I'll be right.

VOICE: Grady stinks like a polecat.

HOGAN: By God, you're right! I'll need to get another pillow.

VOICE: Who put the demons on your track?

HOGAN: Skully. Skully, the slimy bastard.

VOICE: Where's your courage, Ben? Kill him. Kill him.

HOGAN: He gave me a tenner once. And an old, thick overcoat. And a feed of fish and chips. And a pair of shoes that didn't fit me.

VOICE: He's got a pile of money.

HOGAN: Where does he keep it, then?

VOICE: Inside the mattress. Next to the wall.

HOGAN: I'll take it and leave him to his conscience.

VOICE: He hasn't got a conscience. They took his heart out and sewed an alarm o'clock there instead.

HOGAN: I'll cut it out and jump on it.

VOICE: *(Mocking)* No you won't, Hogan. You're too soft-hearted.

HOGAN: Well, I'll take his money, and I'll crown him one for good measure. Just a wee tap on the scone.

VOICE: He's got the woman you want.

HOGAN: Norah, you mean? She doesn't deserve to have me.

VOICE: Skully will tickle her up.

HOGAN: *(Rising and gesturing)* No, no, I'll shoot him! I'll trample him under me feet. I'll clock him with a spanner. I'll pull out his toenails and thread them on a rosary.

VOICE: Don't be so religious.

HOGAN: Ah, Mother of God! I'm a Catholic, aren't I?

VOICE: So am I. The Church would have no work to do without me.

HOGAN: *(Quietly)* Are you the Devil himself?

VOICE: *(With clear inhuman tones)* I came from a place of lamentation, searching for the lodging of a hu.nan body. Very swiftly in the dark. From the waste places where the sign of the cross has never been made. From the black volcanic islands where they suck the marrow of men —

HOGAN begins to cross himself.

Don't cross yourself, Hogan. It's a superstitious habit. I am a traveller looking for human shelter. You cannot imagine the pain of light for such as I am.

HOGAN: What do you want from me?

VOICE: A room to rest in, Hogan. I want to be your guest.

HOGAN: What will you give me if I take you in?

VOICE: Banknotes, Hogan. Banknotes in your pocket. Twenty cases of McCallums. A woman with a belly like a haystack. You can search for needles there till the cows come home.

HOGAN: What else?

VOICE: Revenge. Revenge on Skully.

HOGAN: All right. You be my guest. But no bloody nonsense.

VOICE: Take out your rosary. And your crucifix. Throw them on the floor behind you.

HOGAN: Oh, no! Oh, no!

VOICE: No one can see you doing it. They're just bits of glass and wood.

HOGAN throws the sacramentals behind him.

VOICE: Now kneel down and worship me!

HOGAN kneels to the lighted skull. The light fades out. Pause. Then SKULLY enters and finds HOGAN kneeling.

SKULLY: Sorry, Ben. I didn't know you were saying your prayers.

He bends over HOGAN. HOGAN reaches up and seizes him by the throat.

SKULLY: *(Struggling)* Let go. Let go. You bloody Irish ape! You're choking me. *(He breaks free.)* What's wrong, Ben? Have you gone mad? *(HOGAN circles round him.)*

HOGAN: *(In a clear inhuman voice)* I cannot kill your soul but I destroy your body. *(HOGAN need not move his lips: the 'voice from the skull' may quite well continue.)*

SKULLY: Don't be a fool, Ben. What are you mad at me for? I never told the johns a thing.

HOGAN: *(With same voice)* There is too much brightness in you.

SKULLY: Help! Help! Hogan's gone mad. *(He seizes the bottle from the table and brandishes it.)* Come on Hogan, me boy. If you want a hammering, I'm here to give it to you. *(HOGAN leaps at him and wrenches the bottle away.)* You poor mad ape! God help you, Hogan. *(HOGAN hits him with the bottle. SKULLY falls. HOGAN bashes at his head and shoulders again and again.)*

SKULLY: God! God! *(Dies on the floor.)*

HOGAN goes into bedroom, slashes mattress, removes bank-notes, sticks them in his pockets. He emerges again, picks up the skull and places it on top of SKULLY's body.

HOGAN: Goodbye, hypocrite! *(He pokes the body with his toe. Pause. Then sound of knocking. HOGAN withdraws to bedroom.)* **Et venit agmen muscarum.** And then there came an army of flies.

TED: Skully. Skully. I've brought you a packet of Park Drive. *(He enters.)* Skully, are you there?

TED goes round the stage, sees the body.

TED: Suffering Moses! The old bugger's dead. *(He bends over the body, then stands up again.)* You've had it, Skully. Someone's given you a free ticket to the moon. You can't ride a tiger and never fall off. I'm going to miss you, Skully. *(Pause.)* By God, they'll reckon I've done it! *(He hurries to the door and collides with EILA.)*

TED: I'm sorry. Oh, it's you! *(He holds her arm.)*

EILA: I thought I might find you here. Did you know — Of course you did! It was you that told him. Look, I've brought him some flowers. Blue and yellow irises.

TED: He struck a different double today. *(She moves to go in.)* Don't go in. He's dead.

EILA: Dead? He can't be dead. *(She tears away from TED, runs into the room, sees the body.)* Oh! *(She runs back to TED and weeps. He embraces her.)*

TED: Don't cry, honey. Don't cry. It's all over now. The poor old ram! Someone must have done him in for his money. I'll bet it was that drunken bastard Hogan.

EILA: Don't go! Don't go! Don't leave me alone with him.

TED: I bought him some tobacco. Tobacco and flowers. We both had the same idea —

FATHER TOM enters through the open door.

TED: Who the hell's that? Keep back! *(He pushes EILA behind him.)* It's all right. It's the priest.

FR. TOM: Skully, I'm soaked to the bone. It's too wet a night for walking. Where are you, Skully? I've taken Norah —

TED: He's dead. Take a look at him.

FR. TOM: Dead? Skully dead? He wasn't ready to die — *(He bends over the body, picks up the skull, holds it in his hand.)* Go and ring the police, boy. It's no natural death. Go and ring them quick. I'll stay here with him. There's a phone box at the corner.

TED: Come along, kid. *(They go out holding hands. EILA drops her flowers to the floor.)*

FR. TOM: There's a wrong smell in this house. *(To the skull.)* Did you kill him? I wouldn't put it past you. *(He puts the skull back on the table.)* You'll need a prayer in the place you're at now, Skully. *(He makes the sign of the cross above the body.)* Hail Holy Queen, mother of mercy —

MA BAILEY enters. She has a coat on her arm.

MA BAILEY: Here you are, Mr Skully. Though you don't deserve it. I've mended it as well as I could. It needed a lot of brushing. *(To FATHER TOM.)* I'm sorry. I didn't see you. Where's Mr Skully?

FR. TOM: In another place.

MA BAILEY: *(Seeing SKULLY's body)* Oh! Skully! Skully! What have they done to you? What have they done to you? *(She runs to the body, kneels beside it, puts her head on SKULLY's chest and sobs. The stage darkens.)*

FR. TOM: Hail Holy Queen, mother of mercy, our light, our sweetness and our hope! To thee do we cry, poor banished

100

children of Eve, to thee do we send up our sighs, mourning and weeping in this valley of tears. Turn then, most gracious advocate, thine eyes of mercy towards us, and after this our exile . . . *(HOGAN emerges: confronts FATHER TOM: shambles out: FATHER TOM begins again.)* . . . and after this our exile show unto us the blessed fruit of thy womb, Jesus. O clement, O loving, O sweet Virgin Mary! Pray for us, O holy Mother of God, that we may be worthy of the promises of Christ.

CURTAIN

A nuclear war has destroyed most of the world. Three survivors are living in a wrecked department store: a woman, who is queen, and her weird courtiers ... Summarised, *Salve Regina* sounds like something of a cliché, but this is a play which a panel of judges including Harold Pinter and Kenneth Tynan placed first equal out of about 2,800 entries in the 1968 *Observer* television play-writing competition. Even in the judging, there were signs of the controversy that was to surround the play almost everywhere that it was screened or produced, but Pinter in particular was very enthusiastic about it and for some time it was expected that he would direct the television production; finally, he was unable to do so, but he did suggest how parts should be revised.

Salve Regina exists in three forms: as a half-hour television play, as a very long radio script, and as a medium-length stage play. It was originally written for television, and that is the version printed here; however, in the other media Bowman developed ideas that were latent in the original script but did not lend themselves very well to television. The radio script, for example, uses three locations: Heaven (the trio in space), Limbo (on earth), and Hell (the hole the Queen falls down). The television play is set in Limbo, but there are suggestions of the other areas. When Marina arrives from space, she is idealistic, innocent, and with a clear set of values and ambitions. In Limbo, conventional values are confused; the two men are basically clowns, but the Queen appears as a more active force of evil, and Marina, still full of heavenly righteousness, condemns her to Hell. Marina is reduced to bitch level too, if only by force of circumstances.

Bowman developed the Heaven/Limbo/Hell division from medieval drama, and he took other features from the *commedia dell'arte:* the men's names obviously come from there, and so, probably, does some of the crudity of their dialogue. The stage production accentuated other *commedia dell'arte* elements: for example, faces were very heavily painted (Bowman has said that it would be appropriate for the play to be done in masks), and it is quite obvious even in the television script that the characters are concealing their identities all the time. Also, the stage version ended with the Queen bouncing back on stage and bringing the whole thing to a deliberately artificial and theatrical ending; the same mood of ambivalence is struck by the toy gun at the end of this version, and Marina's enigmatic laughter.

There is a great deal of deliberate vagueness about this play. One can only guess how reliable these characters are in their comments on the state of the world and their part in the war. Do they really believe that the world has disintegrated around them? Or are they just hiding and hoping? With the vagueness goes the blurring of identity through the names, the masks or make-up, the role-playing, and the language. Dialogue is inevitably a problem when a playwright is avoiding a specific location, and Bowman chose to base his on the formality of heads of state talking, but often degenerating into a kind of 'basic vulgarity.' The vagueness brings distancing effects, and it is Bowman's masterly control of distance in this play that makes it such engrossing drama. At the start, all three characters are dehumanized, in the process of unlearning civilised values; Marina arrives, and the audience clutches at a fragile, sympathetic, human element. But then she recedes, is accommodated into the other characters' set-up, and becomes, like them, more an object than a person. It's rather like *Lord of the Flies* in reverse.

One of the fascinating things about this play is the way that it challenges conventional notions about dramatic composition. A close reading will leave no doubt that Bowman has paid scrupulous attention to form, but the design of the play seems highly unorthodox. One expects a play to expand towards the middle, as its conflict reaches crisis proportions, and narrow down to a fairly tidy resolution at the end. *Salve Regina,* however, begins and ends in chaos, and seems to come closest to a conventional resolution about three-quarters of the way through.

But to talk of a resolution, one must have some idea of the values that are being contested, and it is very difficult indeed to pin-point a network of themes and values in this play. Obviously, survival matters to them all, and sex seems a general motivational issue — but what else? Perhaps the main theme is that of renaissance, the re-emergence of something after near obliteration. But re-emergence of what? That seems to be the play's central issue, and the inadequacy of conventional values means that most of their previous behavioural patterns are being challenged. Marina retains some features of the young professional woman, and the men still have some vestiges of their former positions. A vague evolutionary force seems to be operating, and although the men still retain some distinguishing characteristics (Pulchinella is a man of action, crude and direct; Arlecchino is less effectual and rather garrulous), they seem to be getting closer to the dogs outside; the women are turning into bitches.

Is there a resolution at the end? Is Marina going to breed a race of bestial buffoons? For sheer dramatic vigour, it was a splendid idea postulating that the human race is to be sired by a couple of clowns, rather like suggesting that the European Renaissance grew out of the *commedia dell'arte* or that Christianity originated from *Godspell*. But the implications and resonance of *Salve Regina* are elusive, like the characters themselves, whose balletic prancings seem half playful, half awesome.

Salve Regina was first produced in 1969 by London Weekend Television, with a cast including Glenda Jackson (Marina) and Miriam Karlin (the Queen); the same year saw radio and stage productions in New Zealand, and a shorter stage version has subsequently been produced in Britain. Edward Bowman's other plays include *Flashfire, Questions of Loyalty* (1972), and *Solus* (1973).

EXTRACTS from the 'Shooting Script' of *Salve Regina*

These sample extracts illustrate the general principles of drafting a script for a one-set television play with no outdoor shooting. This script is from the original London Weekend Television production (May, 1969), and may be taken as being fairly typical — though of course some companies have their own scripting idiosyncracies. In production, of course, each member of the crew will probably add his own notes to his script, and there must also be a detailed floor plan of set and camera positions (too complex for inclusion here). It will be noted that, as a general rule, visual cues and shots are placed on the left of the page, and the auditory material on the right.

The final running time of the play was just over twenty-five minutes, and the whole studio production, including camera rehearsals, occupied about eleven hours. Most of the shooting was fairly straightforward, but four special videotape recordings had to be prepared and inserted into the main tape. These inserts covered the mixing of promotion captions, the Queen falling down the hole (two shots, using a slow motion disc machine), and the trapdoor closing. In collaboration with Mr Bowman, the director (David Saire) made minor changes to the script. Also, the name 'Pulchinella' was changed to 'Punchinello'.

11. 3 _____ /

C/S PUNCHINELLO   PUNCHINELLO FIRES 1.   F/X
and gun.   1 shot

                               PUNCHINELLO: Death to
                               the French!
                                                          F/X
                               PUNCHINELLO FIRES 1.   1 shot

12. 4 _____ /

MCU ARLECCHINO

CLEAR 3 to B.   ARLECCHINO: The French were a
                               notably refined people; my mother
                               was French.

13. 3(B) _____ /   JARS — Q4

MLS PUNCHINELLO
fgd L. ARLECCHINO   PUNCHINELLO FIRES 1. F/X
bgd R.   JARS — Q5 (set)   1 shot
                               PUNCHINELLO: My father was a
                               Serbian steelworker and my mother
                               was a deep black negress from the
                               Mountains of the Moon. Does it
                               matter?

14. 2 _____ /   JARS — Q6

C/S three jars.
They explode.
                               PUNCHINELLO FIRES 3. F/X
                                                     3 shots
                               PUNCHINELLO (contd.) They're all
                               dead.

15. 3 _____ /

A/B   ARLECCHINO: I deplore your lack
                               of feeling.

16. 4 _____ /   JARS — Q7

A/B   F/X
                               PUNCHINELLO FIRES 1.   1 shot

17. 3 _____ /

A/B Crane up with
PUNCHINELLO. Crab   ARLECCHINO: (contd.) And your
left and hold him R.   pointless aggression.

11.3 indicates shot number 11, through camera 3. Each shot usually presents a different angle, and so requires another camera. *Salve Regina* involved 238 shots, and four cameras were used, though of course each camera was moved to a variety of positions.

C/S means 'close shot,' generally synonymous with 'close-up' **(CU)**, a shot taken at close range, though not as close as 'big close-up' **(BCU).**

F/X is shorthand for 'effects,' specially prepared sound effects.

MCU means 'medium close-up,' synonymous with 'medium close shot' **(MCS)**, not quite as close as 'close-up'.

CLEAR 3 to B means that at this stage camera 3 is being moved from position A to position B in preparation for shot 13.

13.3(B) is a reminder that camera 3 is now in position B.

JARS — Q4 is shorthand for 'Cue 4,' as in theatre terminology. Punchinello's bullets are hitting some jars, and sound effects are required for exploding bottles. It will be noted that the original script required him to shoot at the ceiling; the change to bottles was made at production stage.

MLS 'medium long shot' — a shot large enough to give a full-length view of Arlecchino in the right of the background, and most of Punchinello in the foreground.

14 For the first time since shot 8, viewers actually see the jars exploding close-up.

A/B 'as before' — in other words, in shot 15 camera 3 is giving a medium long shot of the two men, as in shot 13. Note also that in shot 16 the camera is giving a medium close-up of Arlecchino, even though the sound script refers to Punchinello.

Crane a piece of equipment on which the camera is mounted, and which can give it various levels up to about eight feet.

Crab means that the camera is moved sideways, remaining equidistant from Punchinello. If the camera were moved directly towards him or away from him, it would be **'tracking in'** or **'tracking out.'**

42. <u>3</u> /	
M/S QUEEN	QUEEN: Shut up and get out!
Zoom out to hold 3-shot ARLECCHINO/ PUNCHINELLO/ QUEEN	
	PUNCHINELLO: You've upset her.
43. 1C	ARLECCHINO: Out there? Again? /
C/2-s A/B	We went out yesterday!
Pan across and slow zoom out to hold deep 3-s QUEEN/ ARLECCHINO/ PUNCHINELLO	PUNCHINELLO GETTING INTO CLOTHES. HE STRAPS HARNESS.
	QUEEN: And what did you bring back? Gold watches and diamond bracelets! Your sense of values is archaic.
CLEAR 2 TO POS. C	ARLECCHINO: I like beautiful things.
As QUEEN moves fwds. crab L. with her to frame deep 3-s QUEEN-throne/ ARLECCHINO/ PUNCHINELLO	QUEEN: Beautiful things, my arse! You can't lose the habit of acquiring. Go out and find something we can use; you make me nervous decorating the place with your bodies. There's a whole dead city out there waiting, just waiting.
	ARLECCHINO STRUGGLES INTO HIS SUIT.

42.3 Shot number 42, through camera 3.

M/S QUEEN a 'medium shot' of the Queen — slightly closer than 'medium long shot.'

Zoom moving from a long shot towards a close-up (**Zoom in**), or vice versa (**Zoom out**), distinct from **tracking** in that the camera here remains static and is fitted with a zoom lens. In this production, cameras 1 and 3 were fitted with Angenieux zoom lenses.

3-shot or **3-s** three people are in the frame.

Pan 'panoramic' shot, in which the camera is pivoted horizontally; sometimes this shot is used to follow a character's movements (**pan with** ...). Distinct from **crab** in that here the camera mounting is not moved.

EDWARD BOWMAN

Salve Regina

Cast

> ARLECCHINO
> PULCHINELLA
> THE QUEEN
> CAPTAIN MARINA PATEK, U.N.S.B.

The action of the play occurs in the large windowless concrete basement of a wrecked department store. The characters live in one corner, crowding together in an area barely large enough to allow them to move in comfort. This corner is divided by a wall of packing cases with a bed on each side. Furniture and decoration have been improvised from materials found in storage. A large metal trap door is inset in the floor in front of the partition. This door is operated by a lever to reveal a deep dark vertical shaft.

As the play opens, the trap door is closed and on it stands an upturned oil drum.

THE QUEEN sits on the oil drum. She wears a cardboard crown, a pair of Wellington boots, a trench coat with a buckle-less belt tied loosely round her waist and that is all. She is about forty years old. Behind the obvious self-neglect, traces of an earlier dignity remain. She smokes incessantly.

PULCHINELLA sits on the floor to one side, cleaning a machine-pistol. He is thick-set and ungraceful with the wary crouch of a professional fighter. When he moves, it is with purpose and surprising speed. His disposition is hard and aggressive but not without humour.

ARLECCHINO sits on the other side of THE QUEEN, playing a lute. He makes a great business of retaining some sort of refinement of dress and manner; he moves with the stylised grace of a dancer. His fine features and delicate hands give little impression of strength yet it is he who has to fetch and carry; his natural aversion for weaponry does not allow him to do the dirty work of self-protection. Behind THE QUEEN a day-by-day calendar and a large old-fashioned clock are clearly visible. The clock has no glass face to protect the hands which have ceased to move of their own accord.

SCENE 1

August 11th, 2.30 p.m.

ARLECCHINO plays courtly music on the lute — which is terminated abruptly as PULCHINELLA fires a sharp burst from his machine-pistol into the ceiling. Dust and particles of debris fall to the ground.

PULCHINELLA: Death to the French!

ARLECCHINO *(Petulant)*: Must you play with your noisy toy indoors? You'll disturb the Queen.

PULCHINELLA: Nothing could rouse that rancid flyblown carcass.

ARLECCHINO: The French were a notably refined people.

PULCHINELLA *(Disinterested)*: Were they?

ARLECCHINO: My mother was French.

PULCHINELLA: My father was a Serbian Steel-worker and my mother was a deep black negress from the Mountains of the Moon. Does it matter? They're all dead.

ARLECCHINO: I deplore your lack of feeling —

Further burst of machine-pistol fire

ARLECCHINO: — and your pointless aggression.

PULCHINELLA: I can accept what has happened; there's not much use in crying now.

ARLECCHINO: She opened her eyes.

PULCHINELLA: That means nothing.

ARLECCHINO: I think she's awake.

PULCHINELLA: I'll up-end the old hag and have a moment's silly pleasure.

ARLECCHINO: You'll spoil it —

PULCHINELLA: What?

ARLECCHINO: — for me. It's my turn. Tonight.

PULCHINELLA: It was your turn last night.

ARLECCHINO: Look at the calendar! Its the eleventh. August the eleventh.

PULCHINELLA: It was the ninth yesterday; you pulled off two pages together again. For all I know it's still the middle of March! Not that I could say or care about time; it stopped, like the clock, when the rockets came down.

ARLECCHINO: Sometimes the hands move.

PULCHINELLA: You noticed? Remarkable. So do mine.

ARLECCHINO: But *how* do they move?

PULCHINELLA: On the ends of my arms. So.

ARLECCHINO: The clock you fool!

PULCHINELLA: — Because one of us has busy fingers.

ARLECCHINO: Ah! . . . Who?

PULCHINELLA: It doesn't matter; one day you'll wake up to realise that the time is always Now and that there are only two places left: In Here and Out There.

ARLECCHINO *(Triumphantly)*:   So why worry if I tear off a couple of days?

PULCHINELLA: Because I want to know whose turn it is; I want to be fair.

ARLECCHINO: It's mine.

PULCHINELLA: You had her last night.

ARLECCHINO: I did not!

PULCHINELLA: Well *I* didn't!

ARLECCHINO: You can hardly blame me if you got stoned.

PULCHINELLA: It wasn't my turn.

ARLECCHINO: Your turn last night; my turn tonight.

PULCHINELLA leaps to his feet. There is a knife in his hand. ARLECCHINO remains seated.

PULCHINELLA: To the death.

ARLECCHINO: Are you insane?

PULCHINELLA: How should I know?

ARLECCHINO: If I said 'Alright, you can have her', you'd get stoned again, because you can't bear the thought of having to *(pause)* — embrace the old hag.

PULCHINELLA: When it's my turn, it's for me to choose. *(He puts the knife away)* I don't suppose anyone would really be prepared to die for that neutered carcass —

QUEEN *(Suddenly alive)*:   Shut up and get out!

PULCHINELLA: You've upset her.

ARLECCHINO: Out there? Again? We went out yesterday!

PULCHINELLA is already getting into his outdoor clothes: a one piece garment of glossy plastic. Over this he straps a harness to carry spare magazines for his machine-pistol.

QUEEN: And what did you bring back? Gold watches and diamond bracelets! *(Pause)* Bloody useless!

ARLECCHINO: I like beautiful things.

QUEEN: Beautiful things, my arse! You can't lose the habit of acquiring. Go out and find something we can use.

ARLECCHINO reluctantly struggles into his suit. He carries no ammunition or arms.

ARLECCHINO: Why don't *you* go, your majesty? He'll take you.

QUEEN: And feed me to the dogs. I don't trust either of you.

PULCHINELLA: There speaks a true ruler of men!

ARLECCHINO: *(Conciliatory)* Her distrust is instinctive.

PULCHINELLA: She *hogs* that throne with her bottom —

ARLECCHINO: Indelicate.

PULCHINELLA: — Because she doesn't know who will pinch which first when she stands up.

QUEEN: Get out!

PULCHINELLA: Let's go.

ARLECCHINO: What?

PULCHINELLA: Now that the tongue has started —

QUEEN: *Out!*

PULCHINELLA: — It won't stop until we're out of earshot. You can wade through sludge and rhapsodize about the sky —

ARLECCHINO: Salmon pink —

PULCHINELLA: While I shoot the dogs —

ARLECCHINO: Snow —

PULCHINELLA: — that come to eat you up!

ARLECCHINO: Snow from a salmon pink sky.

QUEEN: Snow? In August?

ARLECCHINO: It looks like snow.

QUEEN: Ridiculous!

PULCHINELLA: *(Harshly)* It's ash. There's nothing left of the sky. No sun. No moon. No stars. Nothing but ash . . . Falling ash!

Exeunt ARLECCHINO and PULCHINELLA. THE QUEEN sits for a while. Then goes to the clock. She moves the hands to show 4.30 p.m. She returns to the drum.

THE QUEEN leans backwards and retrieves a bottle from behind the oil drum. She drinks greedily from the neck of the bottle. The metal door is heard to open. Hurried scuffling and two rapid bursts of fire from the machine-pistol follow before the door is slammed shut. Yelping, maddened animals crash against the metal exterior. THE QUEEN takes no notice at all. The outside noises subside as ARLECCHINO approaches, dragging a body by its legs. PULCHINELLA follows, gun in one hand, brushing ash from his clothing with the other. The body is clad in a torn space suit: the head is enclosed in a helmet and the face protected by a perspex visor which is badly cracked.

QUEEN: What the hell have you got there?

ARLECCHINO: We think it's a girl.

QUEEN: Take it out. It's of no use to us.

113

PULCHINELLA: We could eat it.

ARLECCHINO is kneeling by the body; he manages to remove the headpiece. THE QUEEN puts the bottle on the ground between her legs.

ARLECCHINO: She's alive.

PULCHINELLA: We found her in a piece of space machinery —

ARLECCHINO: — surrounded by dogs. He opened fire with his usual enthusiasm —

PULCHINELLA: — I must have killed a dozen or more —

ARLECCHINO: — before I could get close enough to free her.

QUEEN: Why risk your necks?

PULCHINELLA: Why go out at all, if not to find something new.

ARLECCHINO: I think she's quite young. We'll know when we've fattened her up a bit.

QUEEN: No one is to waste food on it.

ARLECCHINO: We have plenty.

PULCHINELLA: All the food in the world!

ARLECCHINO *(Excited)*: Pulchi — Pulchinella! This one may — may be intact!

QUEEN: God forbid!

ARLECCHINO: I don't think He forbids that kind of thing. Imagine the joy of a real nubile woman!

QUEEN: Mankind is finished!

PULCHINELLA: By Royal Decree!

QUEEN: Why didn't you leave her to die. No one invited her. Get her out of here!

The body stirs. Her hair is short and tousled. Her face gaunt and grimy. This is CAPTAIN MARINA PATEK. She is dazed and disorientated at first but she is naturally fit and alert. She recovers appreciably as the scene progresses and has assessed her new circumstances before its close.

MARINA: Where am I?

ARLECCHINO: In an oasis of good fortune, concealed in the lap of Nemesis.

MARINA: Where . . .

PULCHINELLA: There's no longer any conventional answer to your question.

MARINA: How — how is it that you are still alive?

QUEEN *(Sweetly)*: We knew it was going to happen.

PULCHINELLA: We knew *when* it was going to happen.

ARLECCHINO: All three of us.

114

QUEEN: We decided when it would happen and who would press the button . . . Until you appeared we believed that no one else was left. Who *are* you?

MARINA: Captain Marina Patek, United Nations Space Brigade.

QUEEN: Open skies and all that rubbish! . . . Well, child, it didn't work, did it? . . . Where are the rest?

MARINA: The rest?

QUEEN: They didn't turn you loose in the heavens on your own, did they?

MARINA: There are . . . two men still *up*; there's no way *down* for them. I took the chariot.

QUEEN: You took what?

MARINA: The chariot. The escape-module.

ARLECCHINO: You stole it?

PULCHINELLA: Admirable!

MARINA: They were happy to have me go.

QUEEN: Did you really want to come back?

MARINA: I didn't see any future in staying up.

QUEEN: Good heavens, child! What future do you see here?

MARINA: Even a bad future is better than none at all.

QUEEN: But there's nothing here either. We are the dying whimper. What is the difference between a dead satellite and a sterile planet?

PULCHINELLA *(Brightly)*: Is that a riddle?

ARLECCHINO: She doesn't expect an answer.

PULCHINELLA: Then why ask?

QUEEN: Well my dear, what are your plans for the future?

MARINA: Plans? . . . I plan to stay alive . . . and then we must work out some way of starting over again —

QUEEN: We? Start again? So soon? *We* have just finished destroying it all.

MARINA: Can I have a drink?

QUEEN: Don't give her one.

ARLECCHINO: Of course you may; we have plenty.

PULCHINELLA: We could not have survived without.

ARLECCHINO puts the bottle to MARINA's lips. MARINA coughs and splutters.

QUEEN: You're pampering her.

PULCHINELLA: That's put some colour in her cheeks.

QUEEN: Treacherous bastards!

PULCHINELLA: Treason she cries! The old hag will chop off our heads! Proceed with caution Arlecchino.

ARLECCHINO: Of course. One would not wish to die so young, my dear Pulchinella, when life holds so much for us.

MARINA: Those aren't your real names.

PULCHINELLA: Where are the records to prove otherwise?

MARINA: I know your faces.

ARLECCHINO: Don't think about it. You might come to some disturbing conclusions.

MARINA: Who is she?

QUEEN: I am your Queen and these are my fools.

MARINA: Queen of where?

QUEEN: The whole world!

PULCHINELLA: A sort of burnt out status symbol.

MARINA: I've seen her face before.

QUEEN: Undoubtedly —

ARLECCHINO: — on postage stamps.

PULCHINELLA: It is of no consequence; there is no postal service left. No stamp collectors either, for that matter. What she was once has become so much dead matter; she can't even have children. She had herself speyed before she ran away!

QUEEN: — to ensure an end to the spawning of malignant infants.

MARINA: And if I conceive?

QUEEN: I'll have no more of it.

MARINA: What right have you —

QUEEN *(Shouts)*: I am the Queen!

MARINA: — but not God!

QUEEN: I am your queen, your mother, your God. Remember that my child.

MARINA: And if I go against you, how do you bring me to heel? Will you hurl thunderbolts at my head or have your servants drag me to the gallows.

ARLECCHINO: Servants? What servants?

PULCHINELLA: She means us. She doesn't understand.

ARLECCHINO: Why should she, when nothing has been explained?

PULCHINELLA: Quite.

ARLECCHINO: We are not given to accepting orders, my dear.

PULCHINELLA: We are more accustomed to issue instructions, darling.

ARLECCHINO: — which however, has become a somewhat useless function.

PULCHINELLA: Entirely useless. There's no one left to manage, mismanage or subordinate.

ARLECCHINO: Do not regard us as servile extensions of this ... this ...

PULCHINELLA: Royal sepulchre.

ARLECCHINO: Thank you.

PULCHINELLA: My pleasure.

ARLECCHINO: You observe this wall of packing cases? He sleeps on one side. I sleep on the other. *We* are established. But where does the Queen sleep?

MARINA: Where *does* the Queen sleep?

PULCHINELLA: On one side or the other, as we decide between the two of us. She has no place of her own.

MARINA: But if she is Queen —

ARLECCHINO: Oh, she is. She is.

PULCHINELLA: Since there is only one of her and two of us, she is the Queen. Let me explain . . . When it was all over, and she found that she alone, of all her stinking breed, had survived, she settled like a fly on this derelict world, this pile of steaming dung — that's why she wears gumboots. Notice that they are not very clean. 'I am Queen of this monstrous globe of shit', she says. Why? Because it is large, looks important and she's lost her sense of smell.

ARLECCHINO: But you, my angel, have upset the balance of power.

QUEEN: She's a bloody disaster.

PULCHINELLA: Not so fast, old Queen.

ARLECCHINO: We must have time to think.

MARINA: May I expect to know, in due course, how I fit into your pattern of things?

QUEEN *(Icily)*:   You do *not* fit —

PULCHINELLA: Rest assured that we'll let you know, darling.

THE QUEEN stands menacingly over MARINA. She is filled with a quivering white anger. Her voice is cold and very clear.

QUEEN: — and if you cross me, girl, I'll smash you to a bleeding pulp.

PULCHINELLA and ARLECCHINO appear to find this threat extremely amusing.

Tableau freezes.

Black out

SCENE TWO

August 13th, 2.30 p.m.

MARINA has made a complete recovery and it is apparent that she is a well built and good looking young woman.

THE QUEEN is watching MARINA, irritated and a little envious.

QUEEN: It's rubbish.
MARINA: Did you speak?
QUEEN: All you need is a sack to cover your dirty nakedness.

MARINA picks up a long string of pearls.

MARINA: Priceless!
QUEEN: Worthless!

MARINA loops the pearls around her neck.

QUEEN: The place is littered with jewellery . . . What seduction are you planning with all this trash?
MARINA: Where are the men?
QUEEN: I sent them out.
MARINA: Isn't it dangerous?
QUEEN: I expect so. The bickering gets on my nerves.
MARINA: One day they may not come back.
QUEEN: They'll come to an end like everything else.
MARINA: Doesn't it concern you?
QUEEN: Should it? They're animals. What was it like in the space ship?
MARINA: What was what like?
QUEEN: Don't be so naive, child!
MARINA: Nothing happened. Nothing ever happened. We sat and watched each other.
QUEEN: And after a sexless year on the roundabout they cut you loose! Perhaps I should do likewise.
MARINA: I have the same right to be here as any of you.
QUEEN: There you go again, child, talking of Rights as though they existed.
MARINA: Who made you Queen.
QUEEN: Nobody *made* me Queen, I *am.*
MARINA: Supposing that I say that I am Queen?
QUEEN: It would make no difference; you are not! This isn't a party game. There's not enough Greatness left in the world to share between the two of us . . . Tell me, child, why do you wish to be like me?

MARINA: I didn't say that I wanted to be like you.

QUEEN: But you do, don't you?

MARINA: No.

QUEEN *(Viciously)*: Slut!

MARINA: I thought I saw the earth shatter below me . . . can you understand the threat of isolation in an earthless space? . . . But it held together and I have come back alive.

QUEEN: Because you have just returned from the stars, do you imagine that some sort of celestial gold dust has rubbed off on you?

THE QUEEN dismounts angrily from the oil drum and rolls it from over the metal plate.

MARINA: Descent in the chariot was an act of desperation.

QUEEN: An act of lunacy!

MARINA: An act of faith.

QUEEN: When the earth groaned, each of us wished to die but we didn't have the courage to take our own lives.

MARINA: A year after the war and nothing but smoke and dust . . . and the suicide switch. Bright red. Tempting me from the instrument panel.

THE QUEEN moves to the lever board.

MARINA: The chariot was quite low before I saw gaps in the cloud. There was water beneath, then land, ruins of cities, and here and there, patches of green. I decided not to press the switch.

THE QUEEN operates the lever and a large deep hole is uncovered.

QUEEN: And down there? What do you see down there?

MARINA: Nothing.

QUEEN: Nothing. Yes, nothing but darkness. Down there I decayed. I decomposed. Down there is my coffin. There's nothing left of me, girl. Nothing left for you to destroy.

MARINA: Why show me?

QUEEN: To subdue your pride.

MARINA: Rot!

QUEEN: Don't rubbish me, girl. I'll have you down there yet.

MARINA: Will you? How?

QUEEN: Don't treat me lightly.

MARINA: Everyone else does.

QUEEN: Oh, no. You don't understand. It is I . . . *I* who control. Always. Be bloody sure of *that!*

MARINA *(Under her breath)*: Pontificating wind-bag!

QUEEN: And you can drop this comfortable fiction of rockets and space-travel.

MARINA: Comfortable! Sweet Jesus!

QUEEN: Here we live a harder fantasy —

MARINA: *Don't* we.

QUEEN: — more capricious and not so clean.

MARINA: I'm neither blind nor deaf. What's it for?

QUEEN: What?

MARINA: This hole.

QUEEN: Down there ... down there you could learn the sweet taste of death.

MARINA: What *is it* for?

QUEEN: I forget. It served its purpose.

MARINA: It's sick, isn't it?

QUEEN: As deep and purposeless as the chasm between my thighs.

MARINA: And you're so proud. Proud of what you've done. All three of you.

Pause

QUEEN: For all your Sunday-school manners, you provoke them. I see them watching you —

MARINA: There's nothing else to look at.

QUEEN: — watching you wriggle that baby's bottom like a whore at a christening.

MARINA: You haven't answered my question.

QUEEN: I don't have to. Before you burst in on us —

MARINA: I didn't ask to be brought here.

QUEEN: — there was no competition —

MARINA *(Sarcastic)*: Is there now?

QUEEN: — and I don't intend to let you make any difference.

MARINA: She's jealous.

QUEEN: I'm not going to decorate my person with gold, glass and pigmented fat. No! Nor parade naked —

MARINA: Thank God!

QUEEN: — in front of *them* — just because *you* lack confidence in the authority of your own body.

MARINA: Oh ... Do I?

QUEEN *(Becoming very angry)*: I'll let them do it. What they want to do to you ... and I'll watch. When ... When your time comes. I shan't lift a finger. I'll sit here and laugh when you cry out ... when you scream ... then you'll know which of us —

MARINA: Shut your bloody face!

QUEEN: As you struggle for life ... as you fight not to die in the dirt —·
MARINA: Shut up!
QUEEN: — and blood —
MARINA: You don't bloody well know!
QUEEN: You'll learn which of us was right!
MARINA: Never! For God's sake! *No!*
QUEEN: And when you drop that precious child —

MARINA puts her hands over her ears, shuts her eyes tight.

QUEEN: Hear me, you bitch! ... I'll make you listen!

THE QUEEN pulls MARINA's hands away from her ears. MARINA opens her eyes. Spits in THE QUEEN's face.

MARINA: Don't touch me! Don't lay a bloody finger on me!
QUEEN: And when you drop that darling little bundle — are you listening? — when you drop it — one of my perverted baboons will have been its — *daddy*. Tell me —
MARINA: I won't speak!
QUEEN: Tell me this. Can you expect —
MARINA: Foul-mouthed bloody whore!
QUEEN: Can you expect your baby —
MARINA *(Screams)*: No! No! No!
QUEEN: Your baby to be *human?*

MARINA erupts. Slaps THE QUEEN's face sharply.

QUEEN: You ... You ... how ... how? You wouldn't dare!
MARINA *(Snarls)*: I told you! I told you to shut your face! I told you. Whore! Bastard — bitch! —
QUEEN *(Shrill)*: I am the Queen!
MARINA *(Mimics)*: 'I am the Queen. I am the Queen.' — *Horseshit!*

THE QUEEN attacks MARINA, arms flailing and blows ineffectual. MARINA counters with a vicious and professional jab to the stomach. THE QUEEN doubles up, staggers backwards, and disappears bottom first, without a sound, down the open shaft.

MARINA, completely recovered and composed, approaches the shaft slowly. She peers down but sees nothing. The cardboard crown has fallen by the edge. MARINA sighs, picks it up and places it on her head. She smiles to herself and goes to the clock (this, now, is her prerogative). She moves the hands from 2.30 to 4.30.

121

The pit remains uncovered. MARINA stands with her back to the audience. She leans against the oil drum, pressing the outstretched fingers of each hand on the top as though to test its strength. She reaches behind the drum for the bottle and sips surreptitiously. The metal door is heard to open. There are two sharp bursts of machine pistol fire and the door slams shut. She drops the bottle. Maddened yelping animals fling themselves at the metal exterior. PULCHINELLA enters followed by ARLECCHINO who carries festoons of necklaces over his arms.

PULCHINELLA: What have you done with her?

MARINA: She went out.

ARLECCHINO: Why are you wearing her crown?

MARINA: It's no treason to wear a piece of painted cardboard.

PULCHINELLA: Where is she?

MARINA: Down there. She fell.

ARLECCHINO: You should not be wearing her crown.

PULCHINELLA: Why not? The old one has no further use for it.

ARLECCHINO: How can we be sure?

MARINA: Go down and see for yourself.

ARLECCHINO: Down there? Never again!

PULCHINELLA: I believe the girl; the old hag is obviously dead.

ARLECCHINO: How can you speak of our Queen like that when . . when she's only just . . .

He cannot continue but bursts into theatrical sobs.

PULCHINELLA moves surreptitiously behind ARLECCHINO'S back to the calendar. He tears off a page and it is now August 14th.

PULCHINELLA: He's going to pine for the old faggot! He misses the Royal Gumboot on his scrawny neck.

ARLECCHINO *(Recovered)*: What shall we do with her?

MARINA: Do with me?

ARLECCHINO: She *did* kill her, didn't she?

PULCHINELLA: Of course.

MARINA: She hit me. I hit back. She staggered and fell.

PULCHINELLA: A little fiction, a little fact. Splendid economy! Darling, you should have joined us before all this began.

ARLECCHINO: You accept the girl?

PULCHINELLA: Why not? The old one was wearing out; sooner or later we would have had to discard her.

ARLECCHINO: That's true. Very well then, we'll leave the matter at that. *(A pause and then suddenly)* I'll have her tonight.

PULCHINELLA: Not so fast!

ARLECCHINO: It was to have been my turn with . . .

PULCHINELLA: Look at the calendar!

ARLECCHINO *(Cheerfully)*:   Deceitful rat! Not that it matters; dates and times mean nothing and this is a new prize. I'll toss a coin.

PULCHINELLA has his knife in his hand.

PULCHINELLA: We fight!

ARLECCHINO: I know my limitations.

MARINA: Don't I have any say in the matter?

PULCHINELLA: No.

ARLECCHINO: But if you did, what would you say?

PULCHINELLA: Not that it makes any difference.

MARINA: You both repel me.

ARLECCHINO: Which of us repels you least, my dear?

PULCHINELLA: Take care; he'll have you transfixed with words.

MARINA: I know how to look after myself; I have been trained in the art of survival.

PULCHINELLA: It's no art, darling; it's vile and dirty to grovel in the face of nature. Survival is learning to eat dirt without complaining.

MARINA: Not your sort of dirt!

ARLECCHINO: Come now, my dear, you haven't tried us yet.

MARINA: I'm a virgin.

PULCHINELLA: There's no need to apologise.

ARLECCHINO: We all had to make a start somewhere.

PULCHINELLA advances towards MARINA. MARINA backs to the partition wall where PULCHINELLA'S gun rests against a packing case. The gun is in her hands.

MARINA: Keep your distance!

PULCHINELLA: Put it down; it might go off.

ARLECCHINO: And that would hurt.

PULCHINELLA: Let me explain; we are not attempting to seduce you —

ARLECCHINO: We are merely attempting to establish a pattern —

PULCHINELLA: In accord with your concern for the future of Mankind.

ARLECCHINO: Just so. And therefore we must establish our Paternal Responsibilities, on an equitable basis — one way or the other.

PULCHINELLA: Which means, darling, that when I want you,

I'll take you.

ARLECCHINO: Forgive him, my dear, he is an animal.

PULCHINELLA: Shoot him and have done with it.

ARLECCHINO: Let's toss for the silver bullet.

MARINA: I'll kill you both if necessary.

PULCHINELLA: And give birth in due course to a fatherless child! That sort of trick went out of fashion many years ago.

ARLECCHINO: All done with mirrors.

PULCHINELLA *(To ARLECCHINO):* Such frivolity in the face of extreme danger is courage gone mad.

ARLECCHINO: If I have a weakness —

PULCHINELLA: And some quite revolting —

ARLECCHINO: — It is lack of courage.

Suddenly PULCHINELLA is behind MARINA to lock her in an embrace that pins her arms to her sides. She clings to the gun tenaciously.

PULCHINELLA: Arlecchino. Take the gun!

ARLECCHINO is clearly reluctant to do so while the gun continues to point in his direction. He approaches falteringly, his hands before him, like a sleep-walker.

PULCHINELLA: Grab it, for God's sake! It won't burn your fingers.

MARINA: Stay where you are and put your hands in the air!

PULCHINELLA: Well spoken, my brave Captain.

ARLECCHINO continues to shuffle forward, eyes closed as though accepting death. MARINA pulls the trigger. There is a dull pop! A flag appears at the muzzle and on it is written 'bang' in large capital letters. ARLECCHINO doubles up with laughter.

PULCHINELLA *(Laughing):* We haven't had such an afternoon's entertainment since the war.

ARLECCHINO: *(Gasping)* Did you really believe that a cardboard crown entitled you to fire real bullets?

ARLECCHINO takes the toy gun from her limp hands.

MARINA: What sort of idiot have you made of me?

ARLECCHINO: We are all quite ridiculous.

PULCHINELLA and ARLECCHINO replace the plate over the shaft. This they accomplish quickly and without difficulty. The oil drum is returned to its original position. The two men escort MARINA to the oil drum and in dumb show invite her, with extravagant gestures, to be seated. When she turns back to face the audience she is laughing with the men. She perches on the oil drum.

PULCHINELLA: The Queen is dead. Long live the Queen!

The men bow. There is a swell of many voices repeating the words 'long live the Queen!' *MARINA becomes helpless with laughter.*

END

Bruce Mason is a prolific and versatile playwright, very well known for his works for solo theatre *(The End of the Golden Weather, The Waters of Silence,* and *The Counsels of the Wood),* and for his five Maori plays, which he conceived as being 'radically different in style and technique.' *The Pohutukawa Tree* and *Awatea* he describes as 'very thick oil paintings in nineteenth-century style,' *The Hand on the Rail* as 'a straight documentary,' and *Swan Song* as an 'expressionist fantasy.' *Hongi* is 'a set of aquatints and period tableaux.'

Mason has a talent for dialogue, but naturalistic drama has not interested him much since his early work; he confesses a tendency towards a baroque style, and is influenced by musical forms:

The feeling of a Bach fugue when you come to the end of it is that nothing further can be said. The material is exhausted, and I would say that whenever I write a play I want to exhaust my material, exhaust it so that it's played out, nothing further can be said or done.

Hongi was a commissioned play; like most of Mason's other Maori plays, it was written specifically for the voice of Inia Te Wiata. It is noticeable that the figure of Hongi dwarfs the other characters: Kendall and King George are used to put Hongi's stature in perspective and faded out when they have done this, to be replaced by relatively anonymous secondary characters. Dramatically and ideologically, Hongi deflates Kendall and the King; there is nothing much left for them to do except bow out. Mason's Maori characters tend to be used as a touchstone to European values, but their own culture is so fragmented that their supremacy is a very transitory thing. To start with, Hongi is rather like Aroha in *The Pohutukawa Tree,* a diligent student of the European ethos. Aroha becomes more pakeha than the pakehas and applies their standards with a self-destructive rigidity; Hongi reacts against European duplicity, becomes more savage than the unconverted savages, and dies a purposeless, ignoble death. The beginning of the play looks fairly conventional, with the characters in conflict over the 'noble savage' idea; then the myth takes on a harder edge and runs wild, leaving the people behind. Mason's control of mood in this play is particularly subtle, and from the likeable naivety of the first scene to the grotesquerie of the closing episode he twists the audience's sympathies in several directions; obviously, material like this is well suited to a baroque style, perhaps more so than contemporary themes.

Hongi was first produced, as a radio play, in 1968. I have discussed it in more detail in 'The Plays of Bruce Mason,' *Landfall* XXVII, 106 (1973), 102-138.

The following note *'Hongi* as Radio Drama' is by William Austin, Head of Drama, N.Z.B.C., who himself handled the original production of *Hongi.*

HONGI as Radio Drama

Production of a fairly straightforward sixty-minute play takes about three mornings, rehearsing and recording portions of the play (these are called 'cuts') progressively through to the end. Often, a complete read-through takes place before rehearsal and recording begin, to give the actors a general shape of the production. Sometimes, a thirty-minute play which does not involve too many complex sound effects might be rehearsed as a whole.

Hongi was produced in four mornings working from 9 a.m. to 1 p.m., and the script was split into twelve cuts. There was quite a lot of pre-recording, since it was our special wish to make production as comfortable as possible for Inia Te Wiata, who was very heavily committed to other work at the time — in straight drama (*Awatea* for Downstage), opera (*Il Seraglio* for the N.Z. Opera Company), and solo recitals (for the N.Z.B.C.). Often the producer calls on various technical devices to give a particular colour to the voice: adjusting the quality of sound coming through the microphone to acentuate the lower voice register (often used in intimate narration), thinning out the voice in telephone conversations, giving it echo to achieve an ethereal effect or simulating a large hall. Sometimes acoustic screens are placed round the actor to make the sound dead and enclosed. Some studios have an enclosed booth for this purpose specially built into the studio design.

In *Hongi,* we placed screens round Inia Te Wiata (Hongi) and Mark Lyons-Reid (Kendall) to close in the acoustic for the coach, but the coachman and the boys shouting were picked up on another microphone outside the screens. The sound of horses' hooves was from a standard effects disc. Echo (achieved by passing the sound through a reverberometer) was used in the court of George IV; this gave the effect of the actors being in a very large hall, though, in reality, they remained in the carpeted studio. About a dozen voices were used for 'crowd' in *Hongi,* reinforced from a recorded crowd on disc.

The montage sequences were made by assembling on tape a number of different sounds from disc on the turntable and from various tape machines, and playing them in sequence on to another tape; this is the work of the technical operator, but the producer is always present at these pre-recording sessions. Finally, the composite tape is fed into the production, usually from the montage tape to the production tape, but even at that stage other sounds are sometimes introduced to round off the whole montage. When we say sounds are produced 'off', we mean that they are at a distance; they could be played in at low level from disc or tape, or, alternatively, introduced in the studio at a pre-arranged distance judged by the producer.

The passing of time in radio drama is usually indicated by fading the sound on the operator's control panel, taking a pause, and fading a different sound up; an example in *Hongi* is the fading down of the sentry at the gates and the fading up of the trumpets for the King's court. The judging of the length of pauses is a particular skill demanded of the producer. But there are other means of indicating time passing, such as the use of a music bridge between two sequences, though this is not used quite so much these days.

Most effects are introduced during production and recording, but if they are numerous and complex a few may be reserved for introduction at editing stage. The tape is edited by taking sequences from a number of tapes and rerecording them on to the final tape. Sometimes, the producer records two or even more versions of a sequence during production so that the best parts of several versions can be used. Errors can be eliminated and all manner of adjustments made. In the operator's script of *Hongi,* we find the comment at the beginning of a sequence 'remove large cough' — an actor coughed just after the microphone was opened and this had to be removed in editing.

To succeed in radio, the actor must be imaginative and versatile; in this way, he can be considerably in demand, because radio drama does not run out of voices as quickly as television runs out of faces. The writer has many responsibilities to hold and keep the listener's attention: he can easily lose him in the first few minutes, and he must provide climaxes and conflict throughout, so that he keeps his listener till the end. However, a skilful radio producer can assist him by seeing to the vitality and momentum of the work. His job is to use, with discretion and artistry, all the elements at his disposal to give interest and colour to the play. On the other hand, the writer who is truly writing *for the medium* will exploit the instruments at his disposal as the composer of a symphony does, and they should be there on the page of the script, as in a musical score, ready to be brought to life: voice, music, sound, and silence. That is what radio drama is all about.

As well first, to point out historical liberties and deliberate inaccuracies, to prevent others doing so. The Hongi Hika (1777-1828) of these pages has only a glancing likeness to the savage chief remembered in the early chronicles. First, let me point out that though his trip to England (1820-1) is historical and accurately dated here, that he did not go alone, but in company with 'Prince' Waikato. Although it is true that he learned the alphabet in six days in Sydney in 1814 and no doubt gained considerable fluency in the tongue, this is a far cry from the Biblical eloquence I have given him. Further, although the interview with George IV did take place early in 1821, in no work that I have consulted is it suggested that his late majesty was encouraged to prepare the completely fraudulent trial against Queen Caroline on the encouragement and advice of a native chief. But the dates allow it, and in my version, it is at least plausible. Greater liberties have been taken with history in the past. What this brief work is principally concerned with is the concept of 'the noble savage' which inspired two European generations, from about 1770-1830. By then, it was completely exploded. Thus George, in 1821, would still listen to a man whose freedom from the corrupt thought of civilisation was widely assumed and, in the reverse direction, many missionaries assumed that the Gospel would work on simple untutored minds.

They soon discovered that some Maori minds were of great agility and suppleness, able to pervert and twist the Gospel to their own purposes, by a swift and cunning logic. I offer Rev. John Cutler as a composite portrait of these hard-working, God-fearing men, enduring tremendous privations for their faith, but, in the absence of any properly constituted authority, forced unwillingly to subsidise the inter-tribal wars by providing them with muskets, lead and powder. (Even Marsden was involved in this traffic.) He did not exist, historically.

The 'utu' incident I show did in fact happen, and similar episodes were a source of terror and constant harassment in the Bay of Islands until Hongi became supreme in the district.

BRUCE MASON

Hongi

Characters

REV. THOMAS KENDALL
HONGI HIKA
VOICE 1)
VOICE 2)
VOICE 3) *Boys of Eton College*
VOICE 4)
COACHMAN, *Cockney*
CAPTAIN OF THE GUARD
SENTRY 1)
SENTRY 2) *English Regional*
GEORGE IV
LORD CHAMBERLAIN/EQUERRY
MRS KENDALL
MRS CUTLER
REV. JOHN CUTLER
SARAH CUTLER, *Child, 11*
VOICE 1, *Mature, North Country*
BOY, *Scottish*
VOICE 1)
VOICE 2) *Roughish, mature*
VOICE 3)

Rule Britannia sounds faintly and ironically. Fade into noise of coach springs, horses' hooves proceeding at a smart trot.

HONGI HIKA: Mr Kendall?

KENDALL: Yes, my good friend?

HONGI: *Ka wiriwiri ahau i te makariri!*

KENDALL: Shivering with cold? You?

HONGI: Alas, my skin once burned with the heat of a matai fire!

KENDALL: We are far from matai.

HONGI: *Ae.* Very far.

KENDALL *(Exasperated)*: It is the height of summer!

HONGI *(Dolefully)*: English summer. *Makariri, ahau!*

KENDALL: You have your dogskin cloak over your shoulders, your *taniko* cloak at your waist.

HONGI: And the air has ten cold fingers to claw through my *piupiu.*

KENDALL: Your good broadcloth suit rides on the back. You cannot wear it today. To meet a king, your best, Hongi. Only your best.

HONGI: My feet are two cold kumaras, thrown out from the *haangi.*

KENDALL *(Irritated)*: Cease your whining. You are a paramount chief. Be at your best, your bravest, for a king. Now. Tell me what you do.

HONGI: Do not speak; let the king speak to me.

KENDALL: Eyes?

HONGI: On the ground.

KENDALL: Head?

HONGI: Bent.

KENDALL: Mien? Bearing?

HONGI *(Growling the word)*: Submissive.

KENDALL: And how do you take your leave?

HONGI: Like a crab. Like a scuttling crab.

Silence. Fade up hooves, jingling.

HONGI: Mr Kendall?

KENDALL: Hongi?

HONGI: I too am a king.

KENDALL: Of small account today.

HONGI: Of small account! I, who at Kamerihia —

KENDALL: Cambridge Cambridge. The king will not understand you —

HONGI: Did I not offer my tongue to your *wharekura?* Did not your *tohungas* —

KENDALL: Scholars —

HONGI: Listen with respect?

KENDALL: They did.

HONGI: Did they not bow with awe to my mana?

KENDALL: No.

HONGI: *Aue, whakarongo!*

KENDALL: To your words, to your mind. With respect but not with awe.

HONGI: Then for whom here is awe?

KENDALL: For the king.

HONGI: Mana?

KENDALL: Infinite. As the sun and the moon.

HONGI: Whence comes it then, this mana?

KENDALL: From God.

HONGI: And from the Prince of Peace?

KENDALL *(Firmly)*: His Britannic Majesty, George IV, rules by the Grace of God and for the Prince of Peace.

HONGI: No warrior, then?

KENDALL: His throne, his power, his mana: all from the Lord Jesus Christ.

HONGI *(After a pause, quietly)*: Enough for this time.

Fade up horses, jingling.

HONGI *(Fading on)*: What are those towers? Like spars of kauri?

KENDALL: Eton College. We are almost there.

HONGI: *Wharekura?*

KENDALL: For lords and the sons of lords. For the rulers of the world.

Shouting, off. Horses slower. Coachman shouts 'Whoa, there!' Horses stop. Shouting close.

KENDALL: The boys of Eton. They want to see you. Our coming was known: they have heard of your fame.

HONGI: Am I a *hapuku,* to be hooked by their grinning faces out of the sea? To be gaped at?

KENDALL: They wish to pay their respects. Lean from the window.

Cheer.

VOICE 1: It's a fuzzy-wuzzy!

VOICE 2: A mayori!

VOICE 3: A heathing savage!

VOICE 4: A bloody Kaffir!

VOICE 1: He's all tattooed!

VOICE 2: All blue circles!

VOICE 3: Look at his gob!

VOICE 4: Look at his ears!

KENDALL *(Fading on fast)*: Young gentlemen: may I present to you, the great New Zealander, Prince Hongi Hika!

VOICE 1 *(Jeering)*: Prince!

KENDALL *(Firmly)*: A baptised Christian like yourselves, who knows and loves the sacraments.

VOICE 2: Walla walla, bully bully —

VOICE 3: Hingenny, hangenny, kullamakee!

KENDALL: With as good a command of the tongue as you!

VOICE 4: Prove it then.

Silence.

KENDALL *(Closes)*: Speak to them, Hongi.

HONGI *(Likewise)*: *Kahora*. They mock me.

KENDALL: Kill their mockery with the *mere* of your tongue.

VOICES *(All)*: Speech, speech!

Silence.

HONGI *(In a thin, spiteful tone)*: As the crackling of thorns under a pot, is the laughter of fools.

Wondering silence, applause.

VOICE 1: Quoting scripture —

VOICE 2: To his purpose.

Laughter.

HONGI *(Roaring)*: He saith among the trumpets, Ha Ha! and he smelleth the battle far off, the thunder of the captains and the shouting!

Cheering.

VOICE 3: I know, that my Redeemer smelleth!

Roars of laughter.

KENDALL *(Furious)*: Mockers! Sand into the wind! Coachman!

COACHMAN: Give way there, now: give way, I say.

Cheering. Hooves, jingling, cheers fade.

KENDALL: I am sorry. That was not well.

HONGI *(With pride)*: And I? Was I well?

KENDALL: Indeed. You mocked their grins and made them small. A rock among chattering pebbles.

HONGI *(Slily)* : Awe? Mana?

KENDALL: Mana. And yet —

HONGI: And yet?

KENDALL: I could have wished a softer answer. The Gospels, not the Old Testament.

HONGI: There is nothing in the Gospels that speaks to me.

KENDALL: I know it. Perhaps only the Old Book can serve you, Hongi Hika.

Pause.

HONGI: We are here, *e kore.*

Distant sentries, bugles.

COACHMAN: Whoa, there!

Hooves halt. Scraping of brakes, wheels.

CAPTAIN *(Approaching)* : Captain Hooper, Sir; His Majesty's House Guard. May I ask you respectfully to state your business.

KENDALL: An audience with His Majesty.

CAPTAIN: Your permission?

KENDALL: Here.

Paper.

CAPTAIN: All in order, Sir. You may pass. You will be met by the Lord Chamberlain in the Outer Court. He will receive you and tell you how to proceed.

HONGI: *Kei nga tutai ana?*

KENDALL: Yes, they are the King's sentries. Coachman —

HONGI: I am a King. They must salute me.

KENDALL: Hongi —

HONGI: Or I will not pass, Mr Kendall.

KENDALL *(Irritated)* : Very well. Captain?

CAPTAIN *(Off)* : Sir?

KENDALL: One moment, please.

Words inaudible.

CAPTAIN *(Off)* : . . . and give the boys some exercise. Guard! Present, Arms!

The one, two, three of the present.

KENDALL: On, coachman.

Rumble, hooves, fading.

CAPTAIN *(Off)*: Slope, Arms!

One two.

SENTRY 1: Some queer feller, there.

SENTRY 2: Set him on a ship's bow, he'd not be out of place.

SENTRY 1 *(Fading)*: And all done over, like a paisley shawl . . .

Trumpets.

LORD CHAMBERLAIN *(Stentorian)*: May it please your Majesty: the Reverend Thomas Kendall; paramount chief from New Zealand, Hongi Hika!

Slow footsteps.

HONGI *(Quietly)*: The fattest tui I ever saw.

KENDALL *(Hissing severely)*: Eyes downcast! Say 'Your Majesty' the first time; afterwards, 'Sire'.

HONGI: You will see.

Footsteps stop.

GEORGE IV *(Fading on)*: Good day, Mr Kendall. Pray rise. I hope I see you well.

KENDALL: Cheerly, Your Majesty, I thank you. May I present — *(whispering, fiercely)* Nga turi! Knees!

GEORGE IV: Never mind, Kendall.

HONGI *(in a rich, deep voice)*: How do you do, Mr King George!

Dead silence. Intake of breath.

GEORGE IV: How do you do, Mr King Hongi!

Sudden explosion of relieved chatter and laughter.

GEORGE IV *(Very genial)*: So your protégé speaks our rough island tongue, Kendall.

KENDALL: Ay, sir. He learned his alphabet in six days in Sydney, Australia, seven years ago. Since then, he has swallowed the tongue, whole.

GEORGE IV: No need for a finger down the throat to bring it up again, eh Kendall?

Sycophantic laughter from courtiers.

KENDALL *(Stiffly)*: Your Majesty is witty.

GEORGE IV: Well, Mr King Hongi. I have heard tell of you. They say that at Cambridge, you spoke your tongue to Professor Lee.

That you have seen much in my land. What do you make of us?

HONGI: Your crop is people. They flow like the sea; like the sea, they bite the land. They move on it so thick, there is no place for trees. They cannot walk far; they are tethered like dogs on a rope, and must be pulled back. If they stray, you shut them up, far from the sun. I saw a man stretched on a rope. I have seen your Tower, where heads once grinned on stakes. I have seen the place where you put animals. I have ridden the back of an elephant. We have no elephants in my land.

GEORGE IV: But you have all else?

HONGI: Most. *Ae.*

GEORGE IV: And how have you taken to our island food?

HONGI *(Wryly)*: *He taua ano te kai.*

KENDALL *(Translating hastily)*: Even food can attack, says the proverb.

GEORGE IV: It has attacked even me.

HONGI: *Ae, e kore.* And won the engagement.

Gasp. References to the King's obesity are absolutely tapu.

GEORGE IV *(Laughing)*: How absolute the knave is!

Relieved laughter, patter of applause.

Hamlet, Mr Kendall.

KENDALL: I know it, Sire.

GEORGE IV: I begin to like your heathen King. How do you present him, Kendall? Is this Monsieur Rousseau's noble savage? Unspoiled child of nature, till we ravished his innocence? Like that, is it?

KENDALL *(Carefully)*: Unspoiled, perhaps. Innocent? It is a wide word, Sire.

HONGI: Mr King?

GEORGE IV: I listen, Mr King Hongi.

HONGI: Do you rule by the will of the Prince of Peace?

GEORGE IV: Alas. I try to.

HONGI: And succeed?

GEORGE IV: Kendall: your man is a philosopher. Why do you ask?

HONGI: The missionary tells my people of grace, of the ten commandments, of the peace that passeth all understanding. I burn to know if they are right.

GEORGE IV: If you burn, we must douse you. Note, Kendall. Already, I reach for metaphor.

Murmur.

The commandments hang above our lives, like the stars in the sky. Our merciful Lord is our guide and example. But Our Lord is in Heaven. Sometimes, it seems far away.

HONGI *(Murmuring)*: I am answered.

GEORGE IV *(Abruptly)*: My Lords: I would like to converse with the King alone. Leave us.

EQUERRY *(Off)*: Stand all apart?

Shuffling.

KENDALL *(Sotto voice)*: Hongi! Be respectful!

Notes of departure. Closing doors.

GEORGE IV: Friend Hongi. You are a married man?

HONGI: I have nine wives.

GEORGE IV: Nine!

HONGI: How many have you?

GEORGE IV *(After a pause)*: Two.

HONGI: Only two! And you the King of the world!

GEORGE IV: I can command others. But not as wives. My law says only one, and that she must be Queen. But my heart is elsewhere.

He sings softly:

'I'd crowns resign to call thee mine, Sweet lass of Richmond Hill . . . '

HONGI: You kept your crown.

GEORGE IV: And broke my heart. I am saddled with a German sow. She has lived abroad for many years.

HONGI: She refused your blanket?

GEORGE IV: And I hers. If you could see her, Hongi! Now that I am lately King, she has returned and wishes coronation with me.

Pause.

HONGI: What does the King want of me?

GEORGE IV: Counsel. What would you do with her, noble savage, unspoiled Nature's child and pure in heart?

HONGI *(Calmly)*: I would hang her from the nearest totara. Then cook her in my *umu.*

GEORGE IV: *Umu?*

HONGI: Oven. On a bed of hot stones. Then eat her and forget her.

GEORGE IV: That I can hardly do. My customs are against it. Nor would she taste well.

HONGI: You must invoke your mana!

GEORGE IV: Mana?

HONGI: Authority. A king must rule.

GEORGE IV *(Quietly)*: A Daniel come to judgment.

HONGI: What would the Prince of Peace counsel?

GEORGE IV: Not this. Not this.

HONGI: *E tika!* Now I can crush Kendall like a grub. I have the word of a King.

GEORGE IV: How large are your Dominions?

HONGI: I rule the north. I would rule it all.

GEORGE IV: One land, one king?

HONGI: One land, one king.

GEORGE IV: And how will you do this?

HONGI: Not with the Prince of Peace, *e hoa.*

GEORGE IV: We understand each other. You will need guns, powder and shot.

HONGI: Will you give them me?

GEORGE IV: I will give you one, and inscribe it with your name. More would be unwise. But the means for more. Take this ring. That stone is a ruby. Sell it. It will bring you muskets by the hundred.

HONGI *(Mumbling)*: You are good to me.

GEORGE IV: It is not enough?

HONGI: When my enemies have the *pu* also —

GEORGE IV: *Pu?*

HONGI: Guns.

GEORGE IV: Ah! A practical man. Protection!

HONGI: *Ae.*

GEORGE IV: Stand, Hongi.

Pause.

No, you are not a tall man. We might fit you out very well. A moment.

Bell, off.

EQUERRY *(Off)*: Sire?

GEORGE IV: Take the King to the armourer. Let him be measured and fitted for a full suit. Helmet, visor, plumes. You will strike terror into your enemies, my friend. It will repel all shot but that fated to wriggle between the plates. Not likely, I think.

HONGI: From that, the Lord Tu will protect me.

GEORGE IV: Mr King Hongi: I have enjoyed our conversation. You leave a priceless gift with me.

140

HONGI: What gift?

GEORGE IV: Resolution. My lord.

EQUERRY *(Fading on)*: Sire?

GEORGE IV: Send for Lord Liverpool. I wish to see him this day.

EQUERRY: But Sire: he is shooting grouse today.

GEORGE IV: He will shoot no more when he hears our decision.
My lord: we proceed against the Queen!

*Trumpets. Music bridge. Barbaric war cries. A melange of
sounds.*

MRS KENDALL *(Fading up)*: ' . . . at Windsor Castle, where we were
presented to His Majesty the King —'

MRS CUTLER: Bless us!

MRS KENDALL: ' . . . who was most gracious to me and to Hongi,
with whom he had private converse, on the purport of which,
Hongi has been mysterious. The King gave him many presents,
including a fine ring with a splendid ruby. We shall be in
Sydney until July 4th, when we sail on the good ship Westmoreland; by the time your dear eyes read this, we should be
within a day's sailing. I cannot tell you how much I . . .'.
Of a more delicate nature, Mrs Cutler.

MRS CUTLER: So soon! Tomorrow, it may be! Tomorrow, and
Hongi back with us!

MRS KENDALL: And my husband.

MR CUTLER: We need him back. The tribe is fractious. Let us hope
that, in the softer customs of home he has learned —

Sudden noise off, running feet, child screaming.

SARAH CUTLER *(Fading on)*: Mamma! Papa! They are coming!

CUTLER: Who are coming?

SARAH: The tribe, the tribe! Fifty of them, after me!

CUTLER: Jane Kendall: be you gone. Make ready for your
husband's return.

MRS KENDALL: But what is it?

SARAH *(Bursting into tears)*: It's all my fault, my fault!

MRS CUTLER: How, child! What have you done?

SARAH: I was down at the sawpits —

CUTLER: You were told never to go there alone!

SARAH: And there was Makarora —

MRS CUTLER: Hongi's daughter!

MRS KENDALL: She works for Mrs Kemp, now. Lives there as a
servant.

SARAH: We talked of our parents —

MRS KENDALL *(Maliciously)* : As young persons will, oh dear me —

CUTLER: What did you say?

SARAH: She said first.

CUTLER: Very well: what did she say, then?

SARAH: Papa: she said you were no more than a slave; I said you were as great a man as Hongi; she said when he comes back, he will kill you and eat you; I said, when he comes back, you will cut Hongi's head off, and cook it in an iron pot —

MRS CUTLER: Merciful Heavens!

MRS KENDALL: *Utu, utu!*

CUTLER: Begone, Jane. This is no place for you.

MRS KENDALL: Good day, my friends. May God protect you.

Door, bolts shot home.

CUTLER: Foolish child! Your tongue is careless and idle. You will bring misfortune on us. And great privation. Shutter the windows!

Rumbling voices, pounding of feet.

SARAH *(Off)* : They are coming! They are coming!

Roar of voices, screaming of women. Shattering glass, breakage. A heavy chant of ('Utu! Utu! Utu!') *runs right through the mêlée. Scream from MRS CUTLER. Voices recede. Silence.*

CUTLER: Sarah. Water for your mother. And a damp cloth.

SARAH *(Off, weeping)* : Forgive me, sir! Forgive me!

MRS CUTLER *(Reviving)* : Have they gone?

CUTLER *(Tenderly)* : All gone, my dear. Put this cloth on your brow.

MRS CUTLER: John! Look! Nothing is left, nothing! There is nothing in the house!

CUTLER: Nor outside, either. All the hogs, both the goats. Even the cat.

SARAH *(Weeping)* : Oh, Tibbles, Tibbles!

CUTLER: And within, the house is stripped as if by locusts.

MRS CUTLER: It has been the year of the locust, John.

CUTLER: Would Hongi were here! Only he can command them. And let us hope that the ways of the Prince of Peace have commended themselves to him. Come, Ma'am. *(Fading)* Tonight we eat at the Mission House.

Music bridge. Excited shouting.

CHILD'S VOICE: The ship! The ship!

MAORI VOICES: *Kaipuke! Kaipuke!*

142

CUTLER: Yes, the Westmoreland. I can read her letters. They are brailing now.

MRS CUTLER: At last, John.

CUTLER: Not even their *utu* could find my telescope.

MRS CUTLER: Can you see him?

CUTLER: Not yet. Ah! Yes! There is Thomas Kendall. He looks older, thinner.

MRS CUTLER: Hongi?

CUTLER: Not yet. Ah. I see a figure emerging from the wheelhouse . . . Great Heavens!

MRS CUTLER: What is it, John?

CUTLER: Could it be? He flashes, gleams, glints in the sun . . . Emma. He's wearing a full suit of armour!

MRS CUTLER: Armour?

CUTLER: I swear it. With royal plumes.

MRS CUTLER: John: what can this portend?

CUTLER: We shall soon know. One thing seems certain: *(Fading)* it has little to do with the Prince of Peace!

Fade up Maori song of welcome.

HONGI *(Fading on, chanting)*:
    He pukepuke maunga, e pikitea e te tangata
    He pukepuke moana, e ekeina e te waka
    He pukepuke tangata, e kore pikitoa, e te
    tangata
    (A man can climb a steep mountain;
    A canoe can climb mountainous seas;
    A man cannot overcome a great chief.)

CUTLER *(Fading on)*: *E* Hongi. Welcome home.

HONGI *(Clanking)*: I thank Mr Cutler.

CUTLER: And to you also, Thomas Kendall.

KENDALL: I thank you.

CUTLER: We have missed you sorely, Hongi. Your tribe has run wild in your absence.

HONGI: They will run wild no more. A tribe without a chief sprawls, like a body without a head.

CUTLER: We all hope that your knowledge of the great world and your closer acquaintance with the Gospels, will bring peaceful times to Kerikeri.

HONGI: *He pukai to Tu, he pukai to Rongo.* Let us render unto *Tu* the things that are *Tu's* and to *Rongo,* the things that are *Rongo's.*

CUTLER: I hope you may.

HONGI: I, my wives and my sons, will breakfast with you tomorrow.

CUTLER: We are honoured, but alas, we cannot.

HONGI *(Grand and offended)*: You refuse Hongi, as your guest? He whom a King has received?

CUTLER: We must. We have no furniture; no provisions.

HONGI: Why?

CUTLER: *Utu.* Your tribe has taken every stick, every grain.

HONGI: Again, why?

CUTLER: For some chance and foolish words of my daughter, to yours.

HONGI *(Calmly)*: All will be returned. And today, by sunset. Hongi can be magnanimous.

CUTLER: Then we will expect you. At what hour?

HONGI: At dawn.

CUTLER: Agreed, then. My wife will prepare for you.

Excitement off. Longboats sliding up shingle.

CUTLER: Why are the longboats covered?

HONGI: A wet musket is a sick musket.

CUTLER: Muskets!

HONGI: *Ae.* Five boat loads. Six hundred of them.

CUTLER: Merciful God!

HONGI: Your God may be merciful, but mine is not.

CUTLER: Hongi: what have you done? What have you done! Mr Kendall: did you know aught of this?

KENDALL: Ay, and helped him. He traded all his presents, every one, in Port Jackson.

CUTLER: Man: do you know what you do!

KENDALL: Perfectly. I stood there, to see he was not cheated. We drove hard bargains.

CUTLER *(His voice trembling)*: Mr Kendall: you have much to answer for . . .

KENDALL: Sir, do you not yet see, that these guns are your only protection?

CUTLER *(Fading)*: No. I do not yet see. I do not see at all . . .

MRS CUTLER *(Fading up)*: I am still half asleep, John.

CUTLER: It's gone six. Sarah: help your mother.

Clink of cutlery.

Sarah yawns.

MRS CUTLER: How many are we at table?

CUTLER: It may be twenty.

144

MRS CUTLER: Twenty for breakfast!

CUTLER: Wives, sons, daughters, elders.

MRS CUTLER *(Grimly)*: I do much for the Gospel.

CUTLER: Is it too much?

MRS CUTLER *(Resigned)*: No, no, John.

Noise of utensils. Clatter.

Why do I do this? They eat with their fingers.

CUTLER: Hongi, I fancy, no longer does so.

MRS CUTLER: The women can eat on the porch.

CUTLER: And you? Will you eat on the porch?

MRS CUTLER: I will not!

CUTLER: Then all must eat within.

SARAH: Mamma. They are coming.

Tramp of feet, off. Knocking. Ripples of laughter, conversation.
Door opening.

CUTLER: *E* Hongi. *E ariki.* Welcome to this house.

MRS CUTLER *(With an effort)*: Welcome home, Mr Hongi.

HONGI *(Gently)*: His Majesty King George IV called me Mr King
Hongi.

MRS CUTLER *(Curtly)*: Then you must give me time to get used to
it.

HONGI *(Grandly)*: I will give you time. *E noho ki raro! Koutou!*

Noise of sitting.

CUTLER: They need not sit on the floor; there are chairs, benches —

HONGI: In the presence of their King, they will squat. Mr Cutler:
korero. Speak.

CUTLER: What I saw yesterday on the beach, Hongi, grieved me
deeply.

HONGI: *Ko te koura kei te upoko te tutae!*

Suppressed laughter.

Yes, you are like crayfish, painted red like a chief, with filth
in your head.

CUTLER *(Furious):* You insult me.

HONGI: You are a good man and I like you, but your doctrine is
false. I saw it, O missionary! I have talked with your King and
we understood each other well. He has only *Tu* to guide him.
Who guards his house? Who holds his power? Is it your Gospel?
Is it your Prince of Peace? Is it your precious Lord and His

blood? Is it the cross on the hill at Jerusalem? You are a man only of words, and they scatter like sand through a net. Your Church is only for Sundays and singing. I have seen the great Tower where heads once were put on stakes. I have seen the posts where you flog a man until he is a river of blood. I have seen the dirty houses where you shut men away from the light for year on year on year. Is that the counsel of Christ? There is only the Lord *Tu*, and Hongi, his servant. All else is fraud.

CUTLER *(Urgently)*: Hongi. For years I have known you and worked with you. When I have knelt, you have knelt beside me. When I told you of the passion of Our Lord, your eyes brimmed with tears. You learned the Gospel at my side. *I te timatanga te Kupu —*

HONGI *(Softly)*: In the beginning was the Word —

CUTLER: *Na te Atua te kupu —*

HONGI: And the Word was with God —

CUTLER: *Ko te Atua ano te Kupu —*

HONGI: And the Word *was* God. *Aue!* I have learned a different word, *e hoa.* And from the lips of your King.

CUTLER: You have taken the communion bread from my hand. You have eaten the body and drunk the blood of my Lord.

HONGI: And that makes me his slave?

CUTLER: It makes you part of His Sacred Body —

HONGI spits, makes a grimace of contempt.

HONGI: And you dare say that the *kai tangata* is wrong?

CUTLER: It is forbidden to eat human flesh. It is a grievous sin.

MRS CUTLER: A revolting sin! A disgusting, heathen abomination!

CUTLER *(Gently)*: Quiet, Emma. This will not help us.

HONGI: And you think we eat human flesh to gain its strength, its mana?

CUTLER: So I have understood.

HONGI: Eat Christ, and I gain heavenly mana?

CUTLER: You will, if your heart is pure.

HONGI *(Slily)*: Manna from heaven?

CUTLER: If you like. But you play with words.

HONGI: Fool! You have not understood us. We do not eat long pig for its strength or mana, but to degrade it! If my enemy becomes my food, if I take him down to my gut and bowels, he is insulted to eternity. Only war can avenge him. If my God becomes my food, I insult him also. Think on that, missionary.

CUTLER *(Taken aback)*: Why did you not tell me this before?

HONGI: I teased you. I set a trap for my old crayfish, and he came crawling into my pot. It amused me, to see you grapple with our heathen ways and try to make them Christ's ways. Harder than you thought, *e hoa.*

146

CUTLER: I can do naught but try.

HONGI: Answer me this: should the Lord Jesus appear to you now, here at this table, what would you do to him?

CUTLER: I would adore him.

HONGI *(Genially)*: You lie, you lie. You would nail him to the nearest tree; then you would cut him down and drain his blood, pound him into bread; eat him for his mana. No use, no use: just bread for your gut and your bowels, reaching the ground as filth, like all other food.

CUTLER *(Angrily)*: You pervert the Sacraments!

MRS CUTLER: More and more disgusting! Heathen! Savage!

HONGI *(Gently)*: Blush, crayfish, blush. You are in a boiling pot, and your head is full of doubt.

CUTLER: I stand fast, on my faith.

HONGI *(Softly)*: Could it stand a test?

CUTLER: What test?

HONGI: This is your daughter, Sarah. How old is she now?

CUTLER: Eleven.

HONGI: *Ae.* She of the blabber-tongue. Should I split her head with a *mere* —

MRS CUTLER: Stay by me, child. He means no harm.

HONGI: Could you, with the Lord Jesus' help, make her whole again?

CUTLER: No.

HONGI: But did not the Lord Jesus work miracles?

CUTLER: The Book tells us so.

HONGI: And you believe it?

CUTLER: I must believe it.

HONGI: And did not miracles happen to your saints?

CUTLER: So it is written.

HONGI: And these were men of powerful faith and grace in the eyes of the Lord?

CUTLER: Yes, yes, yes!

HONGI: Can you make a miracle?

CUTLER: No.

HONGI: Then you are a man of little faith.

MRS CUTLER *(Hotly)*: Enough, John, enough.

CUTLER: Let us hear him out.

HONGI: You know Tawhaki?

CUTLER: Yes. Your *tohunga.*

HONGI: He can kill a man by thought; where he casts his eye, there will be fire; if he spit on a man's leg, it will wither; a dead branch will grow leaves at his touch. Miracles, *e hoa.*

CUTLER: Necromancy. *Makutu.*

HONGI: But strange. And it disturbs your rest.

CUTLER: Enough, Hongi, enough. What do you want of me?

HONGI: My gods are stronger than yours; mine work miracles and yours do not. It is well. We will protect you.

CUTLER: Protect me!

HONGI: *Ae.* And you need it, my friend. Can you sleep at night, without a barred door? Do you want *utu,* and the promise of *utu,* from morning till night? Do you want your women safe?

CUTLER: Of course, of course.

HONGI: They will be then, by the grace of Hongi and his *taua.* From now until I die, it shall be as if you, your house, your wife, your children, all living things that with you dwell, were *tapu.*

CUTLER: And what do you ask in return?

HONGI *(Slily)*: Supplies.

CUTLER: Of what?

HONGI: Lead, powder, muskets.

MRS CUTLER *(Gasping)*: Shame on you, for a benighted heathen!

CUTLER: You cannot mean this.

HONGI: I will need guns to protect you.

CUTLER: You have guns.

HONGI: Not enough, *e hoa.* I will need more, and more, and more. You can order them, where we cannot. And we will give you food. It is a good bargain. Both will be well pleased.

CUTLER *(Desperately)*: I will give you axes, hoes, grain; I will teach you husbandry, how to plant and how to harvest.

HONGI: *E hoa:* we know it all. Once the missionary brought us axes thick as coins in England; now they rust. Guns, powder, lead: that is your ready money now.

CUTLER: And if I refuse?

HONGI: *Utu.* Pillage. Insult. And from you: only the other cheek. A bad bargain. And you will starve also. A worse bargain.

CUTLER: We must live. Emma, we must live.

HONGI *(Genially)*: *Ae, e hoa. (Fading)* And we must eat . . .

Montage sequence.

A war haka.
Volley of musket-firing.
Screams.
Shouts of triumph.
Conch shell (as a warning).
A deep gong.

MRS CUTLER *(Fading on)*: John?

CUTLER *(In a dead voice)*: Yes, my dear.

MRS CUTLER: Will you not eat?

CUTLER: I have no hunger.

MRS CUTLER: You have news from the Hauraki?

CUTLER: He has killed Hinaki.

MRS CUTLER: Hinaki! His friend!

CUTLER: They shared the same table in Sydney, slept under the same roof; bunked side by side in the Westmoreland. Yet something Hinaki said irked him; he vowed vengeance. He has taken it, in terror. Thousands slain, thousands prisoner. I saw them Emma, passing up the coast in their canoes; wretched bound figures, scarred and torn. Hinaki's death was terrible; Hongi swallowed his eyes while he was yet alive, drank his blood from a chalice.

MRS CUTLER *(Bitterly)*: The noble savage. What fools they are at home: what fools!

CUTLER: And we subsidise it, Emma! The Gospel promotes him! He suffers us to come unto him and forbids us not. Of such is the kingdom of hell . . .

Repeat of montage sequence.

VOICE 1: Tell us, lad. Tell us what you saw. Was it Hongi? Was it really Hongi?

BOY *(Scottish)*: Who else could it be? I saw the fires from the top of the hill, one after another, in a long chain. I knew, then. Then I heard the gongs and the bull-roarers. They couldn't believe it here; no-one ever thought he would be so bold with it! They said he'd never come to Rotorua! But he did. All the way from the coast, through the bush and over the hills. I hid outside, under a bush. And first, a thudding. Then a great tramping and stamping and singing. Then a long shape in the dark like a whale, with a great prow going up and up and up. Then splash when they launched it on the lake, swish and off and away. *(Fading)* They said there's no one alive now on Mokoia . . .

Montage.

VOICE 2: In five years now, ten thousand dead.

VOICE 3: Is it extermination they want? Faith, they'll get it fast. The north laid waste, Hauraki, Rotorua, Waikato. Where next?

VOICE 1: He's charmed, by that armour of his. Twice he's had his helmet shot off; twice he's got up again.

149

VOICE 2: Nothing much to look at, for all his fierce ways. I saw him once, at Keri Keri. Meek as a mouse, quiet, well-spoken; just sitting there, wrapped up in a blanket, brooding.

VOICE 3: For the next strike.

VOICE 1: For all that, he's as cranky, cunning and crafty as they come. They'll never get him now: he'll die in his bed.

Montage.

HONGI: *Aue!*

Silence, then tremendous roar of triumph.

VOICE 2: They got him! They got him at last.

VOICE 3: Defeat?

VOICE 1: Defeat! Hongi defeated? The biggest victory he ever had! And the sliest. A slave had stolen his armour; for the first time, he faced his foes without his magic skin. And a bullet got him in the chest. He stood: didn't fall, didn't totter; just stood.

VOICE 2: And then?

VOICE 1: He called aloud to his two hundred chiefs, hidden in the brush. The other fellers paused. Then out of the scrub tumble only a dozen, but they're not taking chances; his enemies flee like the wind; and that night, another thousand lay on hot stones.

VOICE 2: But he's dying? Hongi's dying at last?

VOICE 1: Ay, of a slow wound. His old sap ebbs. A bullet passed through his lungs; there's a hole in his breast and back; the wind whistles through it like a steam-valve. And he laughs at it.

VOICE 2: Laughs!

VOICE 1: Ay. He who preyed on life, laughs at death. It's fitting.

VOICE 3: He was the toughest old totara in the stand . . . *(Fading)* Won't see his like again . . .

Fade up lamentation, keening, wailing.

MRS CUTLER *(Fading on)*: There it is; there's the canoe. See it? Turning into the river now.

CUTLER: I never saw so many chiefs: must be five hundred here, even to his worst enemies. Their scourge and their terror, and at last, the mainspring of their souls. Something we can never be.

MRS CUTLER: We were of too little faith.

CUTLER: And Saul has slain his thousands and David his ten thousands.

MRS CUTLER *(Fiercely)*: We have scotched the snake and killed it!

CUTLER: Now he glides along a river to his death like King Arthur to Avalon, in dark majesty . . .

MRS CUTLER: He goes to hell.

CUTLER: So inordinate, so outrageous . . .

(Fading) Fallen angel . . .

Fade up lamentation, keening.
Fade up wheezing, heavy breathing.

HONGI *(Faintly)*: Is that you, Mr Cutler? Is that you *e hoa?* How is
it with you, old crayfish? Still bubbling in your pot? Still
blushing? And what is in your head these days? How does the
Gospel now?

CUTLER: It will win at last.

HONGI: I give you five years of peace.

CUTLER: Peace!

HONGI: For peace here, war there. That is the way of the world,
e hoa.

CUTLER: You are much mourned. Many thousands on the marae.

HONGI: They eat and wail, wail and eat. Mourning is good for an
empty belly. Fills it, fast.

CUTLER: You cannot eat?

HONGI: Would, but cannot. A *tamaiti* waits outside; five years old,
and succulent. They will cook him later; feed me morsels.

CUTLER *(Horrified)*: Where?

HONGI: Outside the *whare taua*. You will find him there, tied to
two stakes, a skillet in his mouth.

CUTLER: Alive?

HONGI: And kicking, I would judge.

Receding, running feet. A throaty chuckle from HONGI.
Fade up keening, lamentation.

CUTLER: Alive, but terrified.

The child whimpers.

Who is he?

HONGI: The grandson of a chief. I slew him in battle and dined on
his body. I dishonour his ghost, to Kingdom come and Kingdom
go.

CUTLER *(Shuddering):* Give him to me.

HONGI: No. You will stuff him with the Gospel. Better that I eat
him, pass him through my bowels. I would do less harm to him,
thus.

CUTLER: I must. It is my duty and my calling.

HONGI *(Heavily):* In the beginning, was the Word . . . But the word

is not with God, and the word is not God. It is here, like a
slowly filling lake. My people dip their gourds and drink; the
water is a slow poison. Will you make it pure, this foul water?

CUTLER: Love will purify it.

HONGI: So say you. Then take the boy, but do not give him letters.
Do not let him read.

CUTLER: Not read? Not write?

HONGI: Your words are knives; they strip down our flesh. Once the
pu-tatara could summon the *iwi:* one *iwi,* one flesh. Now there is
a new babble; words dance in their heads and they are deaf to
the old cry. Advance! calls the *pu-tatara;* once they would flow
forward, like the sea. But your words call *raupeka*: doubt. The
mind is split in twain. Forward or back? This way or that? The
iwi once was a rock; your words make it pebbles. When we knew
no letters, we knew no sin. The *iwi* was one great force: you
slice it to the size of a man. Words, words, words, and paper.
They brought you here: they keep you here. And sow division.
Your words flutter over the old *whenua* like snow, thick, soon
thicker. We will be buried, and the old way, frozen. Do not
teach him to read.

CUTLER: You would force him out of the world.

HONGI: He will hear the old songs.

CUTLER: Not if there are none to sing them.

Pause.

HONGI: Take him, then. Take him! I am not hungry.

CUTLER: Make ready to meet your God.

HONGI (*With the ghost of a chuckle):* I I dine tonight with Hine-nui-
te-Po. Her *kai* is good; she knows my taste.

CUTLER: You are brazen and incorrigible.

HONGI (*With satisfaction): Ae, e kore. Ae.*

*Fade up lamentations, keening. CUTLER's voice is heard,
intoning.*

CUTLER: 'I am the Resurrection and the Life, saith the Lord . . . '

Silence.

A melancholy pu-tatara.

152

Select Bibliography

Baxter, James K. 'Jack Winter's Dream.' In *Two Plays* Capricorn Press, Hastings, 1959; also in *Landfall* X, 1956, pp. 180-194.
——— *The Devil and Mr Mulcahy, The Band Rotunda.* Heinemann, Auckland, 1971.
——— *The Sore-footed Man, The Temptations of Oedipus.* Heinemann, Auckland, 1971.
Bland, Peter. 'Father's Day.' In *Landfall* XX1, 1967, pp. 258-292.
——— 'George the Mad-Ad-Man.' In *Act* 3, 1967, pp. 9-16.
——— 'Shsh! He's Becoming a Republic.' In *Landfall* XXIV, 1970, pp. 261-279.
Bradwell, Eric. 'Clay.' In *Clay and Other New Zealand One-Act Plays,* National Magazines Limited, Wellington, 1936.
Coppard, J.A.S. 'Machine Song' and 'Sordid Story.' In *Twelve One-Act Plays from the International One-Act Play Theatre,* ed. Elizabeth Everard, George Allen and Unwin, London, 1939.
——— 'Candy Pink' and 'The Axe and the Oak Tree.' In *Five New Zealand Plays,* ed. John N. Thomson, Collins, Auckland, 1962.
Curnow, Allen. *Four Plays.* Reed, Wellington, 1972.
Hodge, Merton. 'The Wind and the Rain.' In *Famous Plays of 1933-1934,* Gollancz, London, 1934.
Lord, Robert, 'It Isn't Cricket,' In *Act* 15, 1971.
——— 'Meeting Place.' In *Act* 18, 1972.
Mason, Bruce. *The Pohutukawa Tree.* Price Milburn, Wellington, 1960.
——— *The End of the Golden Weather.* Price Milburn, Wellington, 1962.
——— *Awatea.* Price Milburn, Wellington, 1969.
——— *Zero Inn.* New Zealand Theatre Federation, Christchurch, 1970.
Musaphia, Joseph 'Free.' In *Landfall* XVII, 1963, pp. 348-369.
——— 'Victims.' In *Act* 20, 1973.